A Soldier Surrenders

A Soldier Surrenders

THE CONVERSION OF SAINT CAMILLUS DE LELLIS

Susan Peek

A NOVEL

IGNATIUS PRESS   SAN FRANCISCO

Cover design by Riz Boncan Marsella

© 2007 Ignatius Press, San Francisco
All rights reserved

ISBN-13: 978-1-58617-118-6
Library of Congress Control Number 2005938829

Printed in the United States of America ∞

TO OUR LADY, REFUGE OF SINNERS

"*Amen, amen I say to you, that even so there shall be joy in Heaven upon one sinner that doth penance, more than upon ninety-nine just who need not penance.*"

CONTENTS

INTRODUCTION

In asking me to write the introduction to her novel, the author (my wife) has, to some degree, sidestepped a burden. Not that I mind attempting to carry it, because, in so doing, even I may be able to contribute in some very small way to the spreading of devotion toward Saint Camillus de Lellis.

If you, while skimming these words, are casually standing in your local bookstore browsing for a good book to read, but you feel you are already well advanced on the road to sanctity, this book is probably not for you. No, this is a story for the rest of us, the common herd—we folk who, when entering a confessional, still find we have some actual sins to confess. Saint Camillus is for us. He is our champion. He could be aptly described as the unofficial patron saint of strugglers.

It is already well know, of course, that he is indeed the official patron of the sick, of nurses, and of hospitals. Numerous hospitals around the world are named after him. His emblem of a Red Cross can still be seen to this day, as those using it carry out corporal works of mercy in almost every war zone. Sadly, in these godless times, even this hallowed sign has lost, by far, the greater part of its meaning. That Saint Camillus had a genuine compassion for his suffering fellow man goes without saying, but he was no mere melting-heart humanist. For him, the healing of the body, or even the mind, served little or no purpose, unless used to underscore the paramount objective of the healing of a soul made sick by sin. As a man, the thought of a wounded soldier dying in pain on the battlefield filled him with sadness. As a Catholic, the possibility of that same soldier dying in a state of mortal sin, and thence sending his soul to Hell, filled Camillus with an anguished dread. He had the Faith. He was a realist.

Saint Camillus was once himself a soldier, and he knew the horrors of war. But he also knew the total abject horror of committing personal mortal sin. He is a true penitent, yet one of a type that seems rare. The Catholic Church justly boasts of some magnificent examples of valiant penitence. The names of Saint Mary Magdalen, Saint Paul, and Saint Augustine spring readily to mind. Yet these monumental figures tend to give us the impression that, once converted, they never slid back. Although possibly tempted, they never once sinned again. They appear to have attained to an almost instant sanctity.

Saint Camillus can in no way make a claim of belonging to such an elite corps. In fact, quite the contrary. He had his weaknesses, his relapses. His earlier spiritual progress rose, staggered, fell, rose again, only to fall once more. But he never stopped trying. He never despaired to the point of giving up all hope. He was a soldier, and he battled on. Why? What drove him? Ultimately and simply the love of God. It is above all this love, this divine charity, that subsequently overflowed and became the life's work for which he is honored upon the altars of the Catholic Church.

So, for us this book carries a lively message of faith, hope, and charity. After reading it, one is left with the impression that if a man formerly as bad as our hero was can achieve sanctity, then sanctity is achievable by all. But it also carries a hint of warning. That is, if even Camillus could become holy, then what excuse will we ourselves make, when judged by Almighty God, for not doing likewise?

Saint Camillus de Lellis, pray for us all.

Jeff Peek

Feast of Our Lady Help of Christians
MAY 24, 2006

1. The Mercenary ❧

I.

ITALY, 1570 / Snow swirled around the two tired soldiers as they trudged along the deserted country road. Dusk was falling rapidly, and with it the temperature was likewise dropping. The one in the lead pulled his cloak tighter around him, for whatever scant protection it could afford, and stopped to take a drink from his flask.

The other, several yards behind, was having difficulty keeping up with his robust young son, all six foot six of him with the muscle to match, but he was unwilling to let on. Giovanni de Lellis had always been a strong man himself, but these last few days of traveling had taxed his endurance nearly to the limit. His chest ached, and every breath was becoming harder. Well, he thought with impatience, he wasn't growing any younger, and plowing into this relentless wind mile after mile certainly wasn't helping matters.

To his annoyance, a bout of coughing suddenly seized him, and he was forced to step off the road and lean against a tree to steady himself.

His son spun around and eyed him with concern. "Are you all right, Father?" he asked.

But de Lellis only dismissed the question with an impatient gesture, and the harsh coughing eventually subsided. With an effort he moved back onto the road, determined to carry on.

His son, however, remained standing still, obviously thinking otherwise. "Father, you don't look well. Maybe we should rest for a while."

"There's nothing the matter with me, Camillus!" the toughened old soldier protested. But his staggering steps and drawn face belied his words.

Camillus ignored the familiar pain that had started throbbing once again in his own right leg. He reached his father in a few strides and gently but firmly steered him off the road to a fallen log. Quickly dusting the snow from it, he helped the older man sit down. Then he crouched in front of him, trying to decide what to do.

Another violent round of coughing overtook the elder de Lellis, and he struggled with the effort to breathe. Camillus waited until the attack had ceased, then passed him the flask.

"I think, Father, we should veer off up ahead and make a little detour to Signor Vitali's inn. There's no point being in such a hurry these days with nowhere to go. A warm fire and a real bed is what you need tonight."

"A bed! Ahh . . . it's been so long since I've slept in one of those contraptions, I've almost forgotten what it is."

De Lellis drank, then returned the flask to Camillus, who drained its contents and grinned. "To be honest, Father, my motives are somewhat tainted. Actually, I wouldn't mind taking advantage of Signor Vitali's well-stocked wine cellar as well."

The thought brought a smile to the sick man's face. "Nor I, my boy", he assured his son with a wink. "Besides, I suppose the inn's as good a place as any to find out if there's an army looking for a couple of spare swords."

Camillus nodded and pulled off his cloak. He stood up, but winced as the motion sent a painful jab through his right leg. Nonetheless, gritting his teeth, he carefully draped his own cloak around his shivering father.

"That leg of yours bothering you again, Son?"

"It's nothing. Just the cold."

"We really ought to take you to a hospital one of these days. Get a doctor to look at it. Should've done that ages ago."

Camillus shrugged. "It's not that bad. Don't worry about it." He cast a look at the darkening woods around them, then offered his father his shoulder. His father gratefully accepted, and the two men moved back out onto the road.

* * *

"Well, if it isn't Giovanni de Lellis and his incorrigible offspring resurfacing after all these months!" Signor Vitali remarked with pleasant surprise as the door was flung open and a gust of icy wind admitted the snow-dusted pair. He moved forward and heartily shook hands with them both. "Looks like I'll have to mitigate my usual policy tonight and serve drinks on the house for such a special occasion."

The only other occupants remaining in the room at that late hour were two more young soldiers. They glanced up from their game of cards, and one of them smiled with recognition. "Aw!" he called out with mock dismay. "Why is it that every time I happen to be on one of my rare winning streaks, you two always have to show up and spoil it for me?"

Camillus grinned and moved over to join them. "Come on, Antoni", he teased. "You didn't think you could get away with a card game without us smelling it halfway across the border, did you?"

Antoni shook his head ruefully. "Should've known better by now, I guess", he admitted. Then, indicating his opponent, he introduced, "Dario Tellini . . . Camillus de Lellis."

Tellini rose and extended his hand. The two shook hands.

"Haven't seen you and your father in circulation for a while, Camillus", Antoni commented mildly. "What've you been doing with yourselves lately?"

Camillus shrugged evasively. "More or less the same as you." He pulled up a chair and wearily sat down. "Only this time, well . . . in a way we've just been doing it for the other side, that's all."

Antoni cocked a surprised eyebrow, but refrained from comment. Tellini, however, shot Camillus a look of veiled contempt. But before either had further chance to speak, they were joined by the two older men, laden with drinks.

"So, Giovanni," the innkeeper was asking, "what high and mighty commander was it *this* time who could no longer bear you two scoundrels in his ranks?"

De Lellis shook his head. "Ahh . . . the very sultan himself!" he boasted with amusement. "The heathenish Turk—doesn't recognize a couple of decent soldiers when they're staring him straight in the face!"

Tellini lowered the goblet in his hand and eyed the two with open disgust. "No Catholic soldier may be deemed decent, signors," he ventured steadily, "who is willing to take up arms with the Infidel against God and His people."

The elder De Lellis, not in the least bit perturbed, dismissed the implication with a shrug and poured himself a drink. Camillus, however, looked Tellini in the eye with amused defiance and countered, "God and His people didn't pay us enough. The Turks did."

There was an uneasy silence, as the two sized each other up.

Antoni knew Camillus' temper was one to flare easily. In an attempt, therefore, to divert any possible unpleasantness between his two friends, he quickly cleared his throat and cut in. "If it's high-paying soldiering you're after," he said, "why don't you join us in Venice? Dario and I are headed there now. My uncle's captain of a barracks stationed in that area and would surely know how to pay handsomely two mercenaries of . . . uh . . . such broad experience." He smiled ingratiatingly and added, "As a matter of fact, he just happens to be preparing to do battle with the sultan's army come spring."

De Lellis' eyes brightened, and he glanced at his son. "Hmm . . . the sultan. Perhaps he may regret his rashness yet."

"Well, Father?" Camillus queried. "To Venice then?"

The older man considered, then nodded with approval. "To Venice!" he answered.

The two de Lellises looked at each other and smiled. Then both raised their drinks and silently toasted their new destination.

II.

Camillus could have taken his musket and shot himself. Why on earth had he been so stupid as to let his father continue traveling in such a weakened state? He should have recognized the signs for what they were and insisted on remaining at the inn for a few more days.

He could hear the hardening snow crunching beneath their boots as the two of them staggered on alone through the woods in the frozen darkness. He tightened his grip around his father's exhausted frame, hoping against hope that they would come across a farmhouse soon. The shallow breathing and faltering steps warned him that his father was just barely conscious. Camillus had seen those same signs countless times before upon wounded comrades in the battlefield and knew with a sinking heart there was little he could do. That feeling of bitter helplessness he always experienced at seeing the devastation after a battle swept over him now.

He knew he should be hardened against witnessing suffering. He had certainly seen more than enough of it in his twenty years! After all, men lived and they died, and pain was an inevitable part of all that. Especially in his job. But for some reason, Camillus had never been able to overcome his sorrow at beholding another man's misery. Even if the fallen man at his side had been a Turk. There was still some room for sympathy at seeing one of those dogs in the throes of death.

Maybe he and his father shouldn't have hired themselves out to the enemy, he reflected with some remorse. He'd never felt comfortable about it himself. But his father had seen nothing wrong with the idea. Times had been hard, and they had needed the money badly. A job was a job, after all. Besides, it had only been for a short while. The Muslims themselves were loath to keep Catholic mercenaries in their ranks for very long. Camillus sighed. Oh, well . . . what was done was done and mattered little now.

Suddenly his wandering thoughts were jerked back to the present by a low moan from his father. He scanned the countryside with growing desperation and was relieved to spot a faint light through the trees.

"There's a building not too far up ahead", he encouraged. "Just a few more minutes, Father." With a final burst of effort, Camillus half-carried, half-dragged him the remaining distance and started pounding on the door.

It seemed an eternity before the sound of a bolt was heard, and the door cracked open a fraction. A sleepy woman peered out at them.

"What do you want, at this hour?" she yawned.

"My father's sick. I need to find shelter for him."

The woman hesitated.

"Look, I've got money", Camillus persuaded. "I can pay you for your trouble."

At that moment a man came up behind her and drowsily took in the situation. Camillus' father, as if to confirm his unhealthy status, suddenly collapsed to the ground.

Pushing past his wife, the man rushed out to help. Together he and Camillus carried the weakened soldier in to what little warmth remained from the dying fire.

Camillus could see that the farmer's suspicions had been aroused. "Traveling in such weather?" he asked warily. "With your father in this condition?"

Camillus thought, *None of your business*. But seeing his situation, he said, "It all started, you see, during a battle with the Turks . . ."

There was no need to continue. His deliberate deception hit the target instantly. Both the farmer and his wife broke into eager smiles, and the man exclaimed excitedly, "Against the Turks? Ah, God bless you! Mama, bring some blankets—yes! Yes! Quick, woman!"

"Sì, Papa!" she agreed, with equal delight.

"And bring some wine, and some pasta, too!" added her husband, clapping his hands to accentuate the order.

"And we'll accept not a lira for it!" the woman assured Camillus in a maternal tone, as she dashed from the room.

Camillus bit his tongue to keep from laughing. To his surprise, a shadow of a smile flickered across his father's face as well, as if he, too, was amused by the irony of it.

"Signor and Signora Rocci—at your service!" introduced the man proudly. "Defenders of the Holy Church! God bless you! God bless you!"

III.

Camillus felt as if the following days dragged by interminably. His father drifted in and out of consciousness, and Camillus was afraid to leave him alone for more than a few minutes at a time.

Signora Rocci had done her best to make the sick soldier comfortable. The softest bed they owned was shifted into a room with a fireplace. Three times a day the motherly hostess tried to outdo herself with her cooking, but her mouth-watering masterpieces went unappreciated. The elder de Lellis couldn't eat, and his son had no appetite. The latter sat by the bed listlessly, day after day, and the little sleep he allowed himself was usually taken in the nearby chair.

Even the room itself seemed dismal, Camillus thought sullenly. The closed shutters kept the warmth in, it was true, but at the same time they kept out the bright winter sunshine. Only one object in the room seemed to offer any hope, and why it should, Camillus did not know. It had been a long time since he had seen a crucifix. And an even longer time since he had gotten down on his knees in front of one.

Those memories went far back . . . as far as his youngest childhood. Yes, his dear mother had done her best to teach

Camillus how to pray. She had told him all the usual stories about the saints and the daring deeds their love had driven them to perform for Christ. Sometimes those stories had even inspired him, had caused his childish dreams to soar to the very heights of Heaven. But then, always, the same thing would happen. His father would return home from this war or that, proud and invincible with his impressive battle scars and fascinating weapons. He would take his little boy on his knee and tell tales of adventure and heroism that in the boy's mind far surpassed the pious stories of his mother.

For a while, young Camillus had been torn indecisively between the two worlds: the unseen world of Heaven and the saints his mother so lovingly painted for him, and the world of the battlefield, excitement, and glory that his father's words put before his impressionable mind.

Perhaps things might have been different, Camillus reflected now, if his mother had not died when he was still a boy. People had assumed he was too young to understand at the time, but he had seen the hostile glances behind his father's back in the village, heard the whispered accusations that it was his wayward life that had caused his wife to die of sorrow.

Maybe she was looking down at them now . . . perhaps from that Heaven she had so ardently spoken about and longed for. Well, if anyone deserved Heaven, Camillus decided, his mother did. Even in her lifetime the other women of Bucchianico had nicknamed Camilla de Lellis "the saint". Maybe she was even praying for her husband . . .

Somehow, Camillus found the idea comforting. His reflections, however, were interrupted by a soft tap at the door. Camillus looked up, pulling his mind back to the present. "Yes?" he called out.

Signora Rocci quietly entered the room. "Poor boy," she said, "you must be exhausted. You've hardly slept since you arrived."

Camillus could imagine how awful he must look. He hadn't shaven in days, and his clothes and hair were rumpled and untidy.

Moving to the bed, the woman peered down at his father. "He's asleep now", she whispered. "Go, get some rest yourself. I'll stay with him for a while."

Camillus was grateful for her kindness. Still, he doubted sleep would come easily, tired though he was. Reluctantly he rose and ran a hand through his hair. He could really do with a drink. Something stronger than just wine. And a card game too. Yes, that would clear his head more than sleep could.

The idea made him brighten. He grinned at the matronly lady before him and asked, a little sheepishly, "Uh . . . there isn't by chance a tavern anywhere in these parts, is there?"

* * *

It had been a long night. Too long in fact. His pounding head and lurching stomach made Camillus wish, belatedly, that he hadn't drunk quite so much. It hadn't been such a good idea after all, with so little food or sleep in the past few days. The cards hadn't gone right either. His usual luck had run out quickly, and his skill had altogether abandoned him. How stupid to think he could concentrate on a game while his father lay agonizing, perhaps even dying, upon a stranger's bed. It had served him right to lose everything he'd brought with him to the cunning gambler with the smirk on his ugly face. The man had derived immense enjoyment from watching his young opponent lose hand after hand. . . .

On the bed, de Lellis stirred and opened his eyes. He looked at his son and grimaced. "You look awful", he announced.

"You should see yourself, Father", Camillus countered groggily. But he carefully eased him into a sitting position and poured a drink from the pitcher on the bedside table. De Lellis drank gratefully, then his eyes scanned the room. To his son's dismay, he missed nothing.

"Where's your sword, Camillus?" he asked. "And your musket?"

Camillus shrugged, embarrassed. "Uh . . . I guess my mind wasn't quite on the game", he explained lamely.

His father gave an understanding grunt. But his voice, when he spoke, was gentle. "Too worried about your old father to keep your head in a game of cards?" he reproved. "Not at all what I'd expect from a son of mine."

It was a relief to see his father returning to his usual imperious self. With a grin, Camillus swept his hand around their small surroundings and volunteered brightly, "Oh, well, at least the room's free."

De Lellis laughed heartily for the first time in days. "Only the best for a couple of upright Christian soldiers", he added with amusement.

"Nothing less", Camillus agreed. But an inexplicable pang of guilt suddenly stole upon him, diminishing his merriment. He knew he shouldn't have deceived their host and hostess.

Rarely did the old soldier misread his son, but this time he did. "Not to worry, my boy, not to worry. I still have enough money to get you to Venice. And my weapons, well, I have no further use for them."

Camillus shot him a startled look. "What do you mean?" he demanded.

"You know what I mean, son. My fighting days are over."

"Father, don't talk like that! You'll get better! You're still young. You have so much life in you!"

But his father only shook his head. "No. No, not any more. I'm nothing but a feeble old man now, Camillus, and you know it."

Camillus was stunned by the frankness with which his father spoke. He glanced despairingly around the room, as if help would somehow materialize out of nothingness. Unwittingly, and somewhat unwillingly, his eyes were drawn to the crucifix hanging on the wall. It took an effort to tear his gaze away.

"You'll be fine!" he insisted, the vehemence in his own voice surprising him. "Just rest a few more weeks. . . . You'll see! Look, we'll make it to Venice. . . ." His confidence rose, and he smiled mischievously. "The locals won't know what hit them once we start dealing the cards. There's still so much of the world to see, so much to do!"

"For you, my son, yes."

To Camillus' annoyance, there was a sudden knock on the door. "What is it?" he called out, more sharply than he had intended.

Signor and Signora Rocci entered with another man, their steps hesitant. "Excuse us, please, signors", Rocci said uncertainly. "This is my cousin. He's a doctor."

* * *

"Well?" the examination finished, de Lellis fixed his ruthless stare upon the physician and demanded, "I want the truth."

The doctor nodded soberly. "The truth", he echoed. He drew in his breath reflectively and was silent for a long moment. Finally he spoke. "The truth, signor . . . You are a very sick man. I fear I can do nothing for you."

The old soldier did not flinch at his virtual death sentence. His son, however, felt the impact of the words as if the doctor had struck him full in the face. He quickly turned away, hoping his father hadn't seen his expression. No point making it harder for a dying man than it had to be by seeing his own son—his only son—too weak to shoulder the burden bravely.

But it was too late. De Lellis, ever observant, read very clearly what had passed through Camillus' head and heart. They were more than just father and son; they always had been. They were best friends. An inseparable team. And more than that still. De Lellis had always been a hero in his boy's eyes, and he knew it. A hero who was invincible, unconquerable. Indeed, he was beyond even the clutches of death in the mind of his son.

De Lellis sighed sadly. His sorrow was not for himself, no, but for the young man who stood there, looking suddenly so vulnerable, suddenly so much more like a boy than he had in a long, long time.

A hundred words passed through the dying man's mind. A hundred things he could say to his son, if it weren't for these three strangers standing there staring at him like idiots. He wished desperately that they would go away. Go away, and leave him alone with his boy.

Suddenly he felt tired. So very tired. He sank back onto the pillow, drained.

"I will fetch the village priest", Rocci volunteered gently.

But de Lellis had had enough. Enough of all their fussing and intruding.

"*No!*" he objected angrily, mustering all of his strength to sit up again. "I don't need a priest!"

Rocci's mouth dropped in disbelief. His wife and the doctor stared at each other, bewildered. Surely they couldn't have heard him right. Or, if they had, perhaps he hadn't meant what they'd heard. . . .

Rocci recovered his speech. "But—"

"*I said no!*"

The effort was too much. De Lellis fell back onto the bed again. His voice weakened. "The doctor can do nothing for me. Nor can any other man upon this earth."

Finally having mastered his emotions, Camillus turned around. His face was hard, unreadable.

Signora Rocci took up her husband's appeal. "But, signor . . . a priest . . . surely. . ." The words died helplessly on her lips as de Lellis shot her a glare.

Instinctively, simultaneously, three sets of pleading eyes turned toward Camillus, confident that he, at least, would have the power to make his father see some sense.

Their hopes, however, were instantly dashed, as the young man fixed a chilly stare on their appealing faces. He shrugged, almost casually, and said, "You heard him. Let him be. Can't you let a man die in peace?"

IV.

De Lellis' strength diminished rapidly as the days dragged on. It was becoming harder to breathe and endure the convulsing pains that racked his body; harder even to get the words out for a simple sentence. His fever burned high and refused to abate.

Camillus adamantly remained at his side. The waiting was horrible. Waiting, just waiting, for death to come and end his father's torments. He longed to take the pain away himself. Yet he could only sit there, helplessly, and watch. He'd never known such sorrow and doubted if he ever would again.

He tore his gaze away. It was too much to bear. He had to do something—*anything!*—or he'd go insane.

He considered walking the few miles' distance to the tavern again. But, no. What if something happened while he was away? Only a wretch of a son would leave his dying father alone. Besides, the wound on his own leg had reopened, and the pain was relentless. He had bandaged it up as well as he could, but the thought of walking anywhere on it now was enough to banish that idea immediately.

Camillus looked at his father again. He was asleep. Occasionally he would writhe in a spasm of agony, but other than that, he seemed quiet for the moment.

Taking out a deck of cards, Camillus spread them out on the foot of the bed and pulled his chair closer. A game of solitaire was the only thing he could think of. He opened a flagon of wine and filled his tankard. Then he took a long swig and settled down, starting to flip the cards over.

The wine was disappearing quickly. Absently, he refilled his vessel and narrowed his eyes in concentration. He turned over the next card expectantly.

Stupid game! Pointless and idiotic! Camillus impatiently swept the cards off the bed and leaned back in the chair. He drained the contents of the cup, his frustration mounting. Then Camillus grabbed the flagon and once again poured himself another drink.

*　*　*

"Camillus . . . ?"

The sound was barely audible. Hardly more than a whisper.

"Camillus? Son . . . ?"

Somewhere in the depths of his subconscious, the strained voice reached him, tried to drag him from the murky clutches of sleep. Who on earth could be calling him now . . . ? He was so tired, so sleepy. . . .

"Please . . . help me . . ."

Of course, Camillus realized, it was his father speaking. His father!

Camillus bolted awake and tried to focus his blurry vision. He managed to find the bed. It was his father lying there—wasn't it?—yet Camillus could hardly recognize him. Tears were streaming down his cheeks, falling unchecked onto the pillow as he struggled for breath like a drowning man. Camillus had never seen him like that. No, never.

"A priest . . .", de Lellis gasped weakly. "Please, my son . . . a priest . . ."

Camillus could only stare, uncomprehending. "You . . . want a priest?" he asked, his voice sounding unnatural and stupid to his own ears.

"Please . . . hurry . . .", the dying man moaned, his face contorted with the effort of the words.

Camillus swallowed hard, and nodded. "Of course, Father. Of course." He rose quickly and stumbled to the door.

*   *   *

The room was quiet. Deathly quiet.

Two flickering candle stubs burned on the bedside table where the village priest had hastily set up the few things he had needed.

He carefully draped a white sheet over the dead man on the bed in front of him and sadly turned his gaze to the orphaned young soldier. Camillus had taken refuge at the open window, his back toward the room. Slowly the priest moved to where he stood and laid a paternal hand upon his shoulder.

"Your father died in the embrace of Holy Mother Church and the grace of God", he said as gently as he could. "You need not fear for his soul."

But the young man did not move, did not turn to face him.

The priest waited, patiently, for a moment, then tried again. "My son, is there anything . . . ?" His question, however, trailed off helplessly. There was no movement, still no acknowledgment whatsoever from Camillus.

His priestly heart sorrowed for the grief-stricken boy, yearning to console, to enlighten. But he knew one could not force another's will. Alas, not even Almighty God could do that. He could help, or make an attempt to, only if Camillus would let him. Sadly, he said the only thing left for him to say. "If you need me, my son, you know where to find me."

He waited, hoping for some response. But none was forthcoming. Reluctantly, the man of God removed his hand and walked to the door. He cast a last look at Camillus, but he knew with a heavy heart that the boy would not be consoled. With deep regret, he turned and departed from the room, leaving the other alone with his dead father, and his grief.

For a long time Camillus remained at the window, motionless. He felt a numbness he had never known before, an agonizing emptiness. He wondered where the courage would ever come from to bear such sorrow. It seemed as if it could not exist—this courage—yet he knew he would have to find it somewhere. He had no choice.

At length he turned around, his gaze drawn forcibly to the shrouded figure on the bed, where it lingered, unable to break away. His father. How could it be that after fighting so many battles side by side, enduring so many hardships together all these years . . . how could he have let his father die like this? How had he been so blind as not to see that his health had been failing for months? That it was more than just tiredness and fatigue that had been slowly wearing the old man down? Camillus had seen it coming for a long time, he admitted to himself now, and yet he had refused to acknowledge that anything could be seriously wrong. No, he had convinced himself that nothing could touch his father, could ever take him away. Many swords had tried, and failed. Many muskets, many blows—yes, even hunger and dire thirst and exhaustion . . . but all had failed. And in the end, it was his son's blindness alone that had finally conquered the tough old soldier. If only Camillus had taken him to a hospital . . . if only he had insisted on his resting. . .

With an effort, Camillus forced his gaze away from the bed and walked over to the basin. He splashed some of the icy water onto his face, as if he could wash away his grief. It helped, however, to clear his thoughts a little. He realized he desperately needed a shave. And a drink.

With an unsteady hand he fumbled in his jacket for his flask and put it to his lips. It was empty. Frustrated, he went to the cupboard and jerked it open. A flagon appeared in his hand, and he quickly poured himself a drink. It steadied him somewhat, helped to calm his shot nerves.

But, no, this would never do. Camillus drew in his breath. He had to pull himself together! He put the drink down and ordered himself to think clearly.

Yet it seemed impossible. He felt so utterly drained. So very young, and uncertain, and unable to carry on alone. He didn't even want to carry on alone! What was left in the world for him without his father to share it? Even the thought of continuing on his way to Venice, to join his friend Antoni and the assembling troops, no longer held any attraction for him.

He glanced uncertainly at the crucifix on the wall. And then he numbly made a decision. The only decision he felt he could make.

Reaching for his cloak, Camillus pulled it on and slung his father's musket over his shoulder. He was sheathing the sword as a soft knock sounded on the door. He ignored it. He wasn't in the mood to talk to anyone just now. He continued gathering his few remaining possessions and stuffed them roughly into his leather sack.

The door was tentatively pushed open. Signora Rocci stepped in, a tray laden with steaming food balanced in her hands. Her husband followed her into the room.

"We thought you could use something to strengthen you", the woman explained softly.

Camillus looked at them, unsure how to respond. He knew it had been a despicable trick to have taken advantage of their kindness all these weeks. He could feel his cheeks starting to burn with shame at what he had done.

"You've shown hospitality to my father and to me believing we were courageous Christian soldiers", he said lamely. "By now, no doubt, you've discovered how deceived you were. I can accept your charity no longer." He reached into his sack and pulled out a bag of coins. It was all the money he had left in the world, yet he tossed it at the couple.

Neither, however, made a move to catch it. The bag fell noisily to the floor at their feet, but they did not even seem to notice it.

"Signor, you're in no condition to travel", Rocci objected gently. "Just look at yourself . . . you're so exhausted you can hardly stand!"

But Camillus belted on his sword and headed purposefully toward the door. At the look of determination in his eyes, the couple instinctively stepped aside for the large young soldier to pass.

He halted, however, at the threshold. How could he leave like this, without somehow saying thank you to the kind farmer and his wife?

"You've been very good to us", he managed to get out. "You'll never know how grateful I am."

"Poor boy! Please, stay at least for a meal", the woman persisted. "You've no strength left to travel."

Camillus turned to look at them and sighed. "No", he answered. "I've a long distance to go. I can waste no more time."

"To Venice? Bah! The war can go on without you", Rocci stated emphatically, waving his hands in a dismissive gesture.

Camillus drew in a deep breath. "No, not to Venice", he replied. "To Aquila." But he offered them no further explanation. Instead, he turned his gaze one last time to the bed, where it remained a long moment in silent farewell.

At last he requested sadly, "Please . . . see to it that my father has a proper Catholic burial."

Then he turned and walked away, to face the unknown future alone.

2. The Challenge ❧

V

Camillus stood on the low rise overlooking the Franciscan monastery outside the walls of Aquila. The journey had been a difficult one for him. The increasing discomfort in his leg had made walking almost unbearable, and he had had to win his only money at the gambling tables in the taverns dotting the countryside. Still, now that he found himself finally at his destination, the young man wasn't so sure anymore if he really wanted to be here.

He threw aside the homemade crutch he had made for himself along the way and ran a hand through his hair. He wavered for a long moment before finally setting off down the gentle slope to the monastery gate. Somewhat half-heartedly, he pulled at the bell.

A brown-robed friar appeared from the enclosure and serenely opened the gate. The two stood facing each other, Camillus boldly eyeing the friar from head to foot; the porter taking him in with more discretion.

"Signor, we are poor ourselves," the friar began kindly, "but I will fetch you what bread and wine we can spare."

He turned to go on his errand of mercy, but Camillus stopped him with an indignant, "Hey! I'm no beggar! Can't you see that!" The second his words were out, however, he realized with dismay that no, of course the porter could not see that. And little wonder, come to think of it.

"I beg your pardon", the friar apologized. "How, then, can we be of service to you?"

"I want to see Fra Lauretana", Camillus told him, a hint of defiance in his voice.

The porter hesitated. He cleared his throat and explained, "Perhaps I can help you instead. The Guardian, you see, is an extremely busy man. I doubt if—"

But Camillus interrupted him coolly. "Tell him Camillus de Lellis is here." He gave the friar a cocky smile and stated with complete assurance, "He'll see me."

The porter, however, was still reluctant. But the stubborn eyes glaring at him warned that this young man would not be that easy to get rid of. He obviously had no intention of leaving until he had gotten whatever it was he he'd come for.

"Very well, Signor de Lellis", the friar agreed with a sigh. "Come this way. I fear, however, you may find your wait a long one."

Not in the least perturbed by his warning, Camillus followed him through the enclosure to a small, austere parlor, where the porter left him. Camillus didn't bother to sit down. Contrary to the other's opinion, he knew his wait would not be long.

As he'd expected, it was only a matter of moments before the door reopened and a smiling, surprised Fra Lauretana came bustling in. He stopped a few paces in front of Camillus and stood, taking in the strong, rugged soldier before him. Finally, he held out both hands in a gesture of welcome and said warmly, "Camillus, my boy, when I was told you were here . . . I could hardly believe it . . ." He floundered for words.

Camillus stepped forward. "Uncle", he greeted him with a smile. The two shook hands affectionately.

Recovering his speech, the Father Guardian motioned

toward the hard wooden bench. "Come; sit", he invited eagerly, pulling up a second seat for himself. He shook his head reminiscently and muttered, "How you've grown! I haven't seen you since you were but a lad of twelve. Your dear mother had just passed away, and you were spirited off to live with your cousins and complete your studies."

"I remember it well."

The quiet words drew the priest back to the present, and he suddenly feared that perhaps he had said the wrong thing and renewed some of his nephew's pain. He decided to change the subject and began speaking rapidly and lightheartedly, as if by so doing he could gloss over the sorrowful memories.

"So now, what brings you to Aquila, my boy? The last I'd heard you'd run away to join your father in the army. That must've been, what? . . . about three or four years ago? And now . . . perhaps some misfortune?"

He did not, however, give Camillus the opportunity to reply. Instead he reassured quickly, "Not to worry, not to worry! A few good meals, fresh clothes, and then, as you know, we Franciscans can certainly ensure you a peaceful night's sleep."

Again, Camillus opened his mouth to say something, but his uncle continued.

"Unlike our venerable brethren, the Benedictines! Now, *they* would have had you up at two in the morning to sing Matins, and then of course—"

"*Uncle!*" Camillus flared, finally losing his patience.

The priest was stunned into silence by the sudden outburst, his mouth still open, in mid-sentence.

Camillus knew he had finally captured the other's attention, but he was nonetheless fearful of another interruption. Slowly spacing his next words, he firmly announced his intention. "Uncle, I—want—to—be—a—Franciscan."

A wall of silence dropped into the room. The Guardian stared at his nephew blankly. This was the last thing in the world he'd been expecting, and he was clearly unprepared, speechless.

Camillus dived into the silence, partially defensive but mostly persuasive. "I know! I know what you're thinking! But listen. I might as well become a monk. There's nothing left for me in the world anymore—no work, no money, no family—"

His uncle grasped at this last phrase and cut in. "No family? But, your father—"

"Father is dead." The announcement was hard, cold. Bitterness was his only defense against the grief.

Poor Fra Lauretana received yet another shock. He sat there dumbfounded, trying to absorb all the twists and turns of this totally unforeseen visitation. He groped for words. "I . . . I'm sorry, Camillus. I hadn't heard . . ."

"It happened only last week", Camillus informed him in that same embittered tone.

The shock on his uncle's face abruptly changed into anxiety, as the consequences dawned horribly upon him.

Camillus, however, saw the unspoken question, and his voice softened. "He received the Last Sacraments, if that's your concern."

But his uncle didn't look entirely consoled.

"Look, his death was good!" Camillus insisted stubbornly. "Believe me, I know! I was there."

The priest closed his eyes for an instant of silent prayer. "Deo gratias!" he whispered fervently. "I have never ceased to pray for him."

Camillus, however, didn't feel like talking about it. The sorrow was still far too fresh. Instead, he pushed the memory of his father away and returned to the matter at hand. "You will, of course, accept me, won't you?" he asked.

Somehow it didn't quite sound like a question.

His uncle reopened his eyes and tried to focus his thoughts on the present situation. It wasn't easy, trying to take in all of these sudden surprises. He felt a vague uneasiness about this unexpected request. It seemed more like a confrontation than a humble petition to be received as a postulant.

Clearing his throat and hoping he sounded as authoritative as a man in his high position should, he replied carefully, "Camillus, I can see you're in a state of exhaustion and in no fit frame of mind to make such a serious decision. For now, you must rest and regain your strength. Then we can discuss this matter further."

"There's nothing wrong with me!" his nephew snapped. "I know exactly what I'm saying!"

But a firmly raised hand cut off the flow of words, and the priest announced steadily, "The first test of any vocation, Camillus, is the readiness to obey."

Camillus clamped his mouth shut, but his expression was anything but submissive. For one dreadful moment the poor priest feared he was about to laugh at his nephew's uncanny resemblance to his truculent, pig-headed brother-in-law—God rest his soul! There was certainly no doubt from which side of the family this lad had inherited his temperament. But laughing would never do. He bit his tongue until the urge passed and managed to say instead, "The porter mentioned to me that you have a pronounced limp. I'll ask Fra Dominic to have a look at it. He has some skill with healing."

"It's nothing", Camillus protested. "Just a little scratch, that's all."

Ignoring this last remark, Fra Lauretana stood up decisively. "Follow me, my boy. We shall find a cell for you."

VI.

The cell was no less austere than the parlor. More so, in fact. A hard straw bed and rough wooden stool, which seconded as a writing table, were the only furniture. The sole ornamentation, a crucifix on the wall.

The door opened quietly and a shaft of sunlight filtered into the dimly lit room. Camillus looked up from where he was sitting on the edge of the bed in deep thought.

"How are you today, Camillus?" his uncle asked gently, shutting the door behind him.

"I'm all right."

Fra Lauretana nodded. "You're looking much better since you had a bit of a spruce-up, and doubtless you're feeling better, too, after making a good confession." Indeed, the clean clothes, fresh shave, confession, and much-needed sleep had done wonders for his nephew. Only the haunting sorrow in his eyes remained. But the priest knew with a heavy heart that that could not disappear so easily.

"Perhaps we should talk, my boy", he suggested.

To his dismay, Camillus only shrugged and said uncooperatively, "Talk away. I've already told you why I'm here."

The Guardian sighed. It was obvious the lad was not

going to make this easy for him. He had tried hard over the last few days to convince himself that his nephew might have a monastic vocation, but try as he might, he could not imagine it being genuine.

"Camillus, really . . . I . . .", he paused, at a loss. How could he break the news? An approach came to mind, and he asked, "How old are you?"

"Old enough to make my own decisions."

Poor Fra Lauretana was in no mood for games. This roguish, hard-headed nephew of his had already put him on the spot enough. "How old?" he insisted firmly.

Camillus rolled his eyes. "Twenty."

"And how long exactly have you . . . uh . . . felt the call of God?"

Impatiently the young man stood up. "I've already told you!" he answered hotly. "It was just last week, when Father died." Then, unexpectedly, his voice took on a pleading edge. "I know you think I'm being rash, Uncle, but . . . well . . . just to see him die like that . . ." His words faltered.

His uncle waited for a moment. Maybe now they were getting somewhere. If only he could break down his nephew's defense, could get him to unburden his heart. At least a little! "Go on", he encouraged gently.

There was something in those kind eyes . . . *something* . . . that reminded Camillus so much of his loving mother. It was too much to resist; his barrier came tumbling down and, in a headlong rush of words, he confided, "My father taught me everything I know. How to fight, how to survive against great odds, how to gamble. He taught me everything. But all that was nothing—*absolutely nothing!*—compared to his last lesson." He drew in a deep breath and finished feelingly, "His death."

The priest stepped forward and placed his hands gently upon his nephew's shoulders. "It is a great grace, Camillus, to realize that death may overtake you, too, at any moment. You must always be ready; you must amend your worldly and sinful ways."

But at his last words, Camillus' face instantly hardened again. He obviously didn't appreciate being told he was in no way a saint. Instinctively, the older man let his hands drop, but nonetheless bravely continued. "But the mere realization of that alone does not prove that God has called you to the cloister. You see, Camillus," he tried to explain, "vocations do not come so easily. It is good, very good, that you want to part with your bad habits. You have had the grace of a sincere confession. You can, and indeed must, make a fresh start. But the monastery is not a place to hide from our crosses."

"But you don't understand, Uncle. After Father died, I vowed to God to become a Franciscan."

Fra Lauretana shook his head. "Our Lord is merciful, Camillus. He knows you made that promise only in a moment of shock, and sorrow, and so you are not bound to it."

There was a silence. Camillus returned to the bed and sat down, trying to sort it all out in his own mind. His uncle could see he wasn't pleased with the way things were progressing.

After a moment he looked up again, and demanded with annoyance, "So what you're telling me is that I have no vocation?"

"I'm telling you to change your life first. To seek God's holy will through prayer, and penance."

"But you—"

For once, the mere look in his uncle's eyes was enough to silence him.

The moment the priest had been dreading had finally arrived. He must deal the final blow. "Besides," he said, "I cannot admit you to our novitiate on account of that ulcer on your leg. Fra Dominic tells me he's never seen anything quite like it. It's severely infected and needs proper medical attention, which he's unequipped to give." He sighed sadly. "That alone, I fear, is sign enough from God that He isn't calling you to our life here. I'm very sorry, Camillus. I truly am." He cast a quick glance at the crucifix on the wall, hoping he had done the right thing, made the right decision.

Camillus realized he was defeated, something he was not used to and clearly not too happy about. Abruptly he arose and snatched up his musket. He flung on his cloak, as his uncle watched with helpless compassion.

"There's an excellent hospital for men in Rome, called San Giacomo. Go there, Camillus", he suggested gently. "They have many good and well-trained doctors."

"And then?" Camillus challenged.

The poor Guardian felt trapped once again. He hesitated. There was little doubt in his mind that his nephew had no vocation to the cloister, but he decided it wouldn't hurt to give in, for the time being. "If they can truly cure your leg, then come back and . . .", he couldn't prevent the weary sigh that escaped his lips, "and we can reconsider the matter."

But Camillus was too quick to be fooled. He looked at his uncle with suspicion. After a moment, however, to the priest's great relief, Camillus' good humor won the day, and he smiled, although somewhat halfheartedly. "All right. You win", he conceded sportingly. "I won't be back."

"Have you any money left?"

Reluctantly Camillus shook his head. The priest reached into his habit and pulled out what few coins he had. He urged them into his nephew's unwilling hand.

"I'm sorry. I wish it were more. But I've arranged for some provisions for you at the gate. The porter will have them ready for you."

It was terrible business, this. Just terrible! Turning out his sister's only child like this—homeless, wounded, and all but penniless! It was all the more shameful because the provisions waiting at the door were witness to the fact that he'd already made his final decision long before this very conversation.

Again, the poor priest sighed sadly. Alas, he knew in his heart he could not have decided otherwise.

He reached once more into the deep folds of his habit, and his hand emerged with a small, hand-carved crucifix. "Take this, my boy", he said. "God will go with you."

Camillus took the crucifix. Then, on a sudden impulse, he dropped to his knees in front of the priest for a blessing.

Then he arose, looked at his uncle fondly, and left the cell without another word.

Fra Lauretana watched him go, his own expression a strange mixture of affection, relief, and a good deal of worry.

Slowly he shook his head and sank to his own knees in the little cell to pray.

VII.

ROME, 1571 / The scene before him looked more like a charnel house than a hospital ward, Camillus thought with dismay as he stood gazing through the doorway. He leaned on his musket to lessen the throbbing pain in his leg. Until now, he had believed only a battlefield could hold so much human suffering and hopelessness in one place, but the pitiful moans and nauseating stench of blood and rotting limbs attacking him quickly convinced him of his misconception.

For a long moment he considered turning around and heading straight back out into the streets of Rome. But no, his uncle had been right. His father had been right. He needed to get his leg taken care of once and for all if he ever wanted to get on with his life. The thought that his father had wanted him to go to a hospital such as this gave Camillus the courage he needed, and he forced himself to enter the room.

He could no longer endure placing much weight upon his leg; the gun would have to serve as a crutch. He took a few hesitant paces and winced.

"Do you need a hand?" he heard someone ask nearby.

He turned toward the speaker, a young hospital orderly who looked about his own age. The fellow's eyes showed such genuine concern that Camillus managed a weak smile.

"I'm fine. Thanks", he said. "Is there a doctor on duty around here?"

"Doctor Moretti. He's over there." The orderly pointed across the room.

Camillus nodded his thanks and slowly picked his way through the rows of beds to the doctor, who was examining a patient. He waited until he was finished and then asked, "Uh, Doctor Moretti?"

"Yes?" Moretti's voice sounded distracted, almost indifferent. Obviously he was a man with far too much on his mind, hardly surprising judging from the looks of the ward around them.

"My name's Camillus de Lellis."

The doctor dutifully shook the proffered hand, and Camillus continued, "I have a bad leg. Do you think you could treat it?"

Moretti eyed him for a moment. "Possibly", he answered with reserve. "That depends on a number of things."

There was no way around it. Camillus knew he had to tell him. "I . . . um . . . I have no money", he confessed. At the sharp look from the doctor, however, he quickly added, "But I'm willing to work to repay you for your help."

The doctor briefly considered the proposal, then nodded. "I suppose, yes, we can always use another orderly here. Someone to sweep the floors, serve the meals." He paused and regarded the gun in Camillus' hand. "But I fear you'll have to turn that musket over to me. The rules of the hospital expressly forbid the possession of firearms, for obvious reasons."

Camillus hesitated for an instant, then decided to comply. He handed the weapon to the doctor, who laid it on the empty bed beside him and said, "Now, show me this leg of yours."

Sitting down, Camillus pulled off his boot. When he did that a bolt of pain shot through him, but Moretti's expression registered no compassion. The doctor bent to examine the wound, then clicked his tongue with displeasure.

"Looks nasty. It's highly infected." He glanced up. "What caused this?"

Camillus didn't want to tell him. "It's a battle wound from a few months ago", he lied. "It never healed up."

Moretti's eyes narrowed with suspicion, and he looked at it more closely. "This is no battle wound", he announced, irked by the deception.

Camillus drew in his breath thoughtfully. Should he admit the truth? To be wounded in combat was, if nothing else, at least honorable. Something a man could glory in. But to be made lame by some mysterious ulcer with no apparent cause was shameful and humiliating. No, he decided quickly, he wouldn't let this brisk, sharp-eyed doctor know that.

"If I say it's a battle wound, then it's a battle wound", he replied stubbornly.

Moretti glared at him. "Listen, young man! I can't help you if you persist in lying to me. No weapon caused this infection."

Camillus felt piqued. What did it matter what had caused it? He gritted his teeth and grudgingly conceded, "All right then! It's not a battle wound."

He could see that the doctor was also becoming irritated. "Then tell me what caused it."

"I don't know", Camillus answered sullenly. "It just appeared one day."

Moretti sighed with impatience. "Surely you must have *some* idea, Signor . . . uh . . . de Lellis. Think back. Where were you when it first appeared?"

Camillus shrugged. "I can't remember. North Africa, I think."

The doctor nodded, pensively. "Perhaps there was some disease prevalent in your army camp", he suggested. "Were any of the other soldiers affected by ulcers similar to this?"

This examination was taking far too long. Camillus was

already red with embarrassment at the unsightly thing being exposed. He longed to put his boot back on and cover it up. "Look, I wouldn't know!" he retorted.

Moretti's patience was likewise ebbing quickly. He cast his eyes around the room. He had so much to do; there were so many other men who needed his attention. He had neither the time nor the inclination to deal with this young soldier's petulant attitude. "What do you mean, you don't know?" he snapped, his voice a bit too loud in the otherwise quiet room. "If you were in an army camp, then certainly you—"

Camillus flared. "I already told you! I don't know!" he blurted out, the volume of his own voice rising. "How should I know what filthy diseases were floating around some stinking Turkish army cam—"

Horror-struck, he realized instantly the mistake he'd made and clamped his mouth shut.

But too late. There was a tense silence.

Camillus knew, with dreadful certainty, that not only had the doctor picked up on his blunder, but so had everyone else surrounding them.

Moretti was staring at him, incredulous. Camillus' heartbeat quickened with anger at his own stupidity. How could he have lost his head so badly!

Slowly the doctor rose to his feet. "Turkish army camp?" he repeated in a stunned whisper. "Did you say *Turkish* army camp?"

Camillus instinctively stood up as well. He could feel the hostile eyes all around him, as everyone was taking in the scene. He tried desperately to think of something to say, but couldn't, and knew with despair that his face must be giving everything away.

"Why, you despicable traitor!" Moretti managed to hiss between clenched teeth. "Not ashamed to slaughter your own countrymen, to butcher those upholding the Holy Roman Faith! Oh, no, not even ashamed to come sniveling back here with your contemptible heathen diseases!"

Camillus opened his mouth to defend himself. "Look! I never even—"

But Moretti cut him short. "You're like a pig sold in the market, going to the highest bidder! You cheap, disgusting mercenary!"

Instant rage surged through Camillus at the degrading insult. His muscles tensed and he clenched his fists, but no . . . he knew he was helpless. Utterly helpless, standing there with a roomful of Catholic eyes boring into him. He had no choice but to take it like a man.

Somewhere in the back of his mind, he fleetingly remembered that he had recently been to confession at the monastery. God at least knew what those in this room couldn't. He felt his anger abate slightly.

It was obvious to everyone watching, including Camillus himself, that Moretti was making a tremendous effort not to lash out at him. Taking a few deep breaths, he managed to go on. "If my word as a doctor had not already been given, I'd send you away now! But as it is, my fine young hero, just one word, one breath, one *hair* out of place, and you'll be back in the gutter, where you belong!"

With that, the doctor snatched up the musket from the bed and stalked away.

Camillus stood there, dazed. He knew everyone was staring at him with loathing, and he felt his cheeks burn. He suddenly felt the need to sit down again.

Sinking back onto the edge of the bed, he buried his

face in his hands. Wonderful. Just brilliant. First his father dies, then his uncle sends him away, and now this! Maybe he should just get up and leave after all. But no, he realized with dismay, he couldn't even do that! That foul doctor had walked off with his gun. And he certainly was in no mood to chase after him and grovel for it!

A hand touched him lightly on the arm, and he reluctantly looked up. The orderly whom he had met earlier was standing there. Camillus saw that his eyes, surprisingly, were not disdainful, but compassionate.

"If you want to come with me," he offered, "I'll take you to the orderlies' dormitory." He hesitated for an instant, then added, "Don't worry. Moretti will calm down in a couple of hours. But until he does, I'll help you get that wound cleaned up properly."

Camillus was too ashamed to answer. He nodded silently and pulled on his boot. Then he got to his feet and didn't object this time when the other offered him a shoulder to lean on.

VIII.

It didn't take long for Camillus to realize that most of the duties of a hospital orderly were dirty, backbreaking, and monotonous. He felt like a wretched scullery maid and was starting to detest the place already, after less than a week.

What was the point in trying to scrub a floor clean every day when, inevitably, five minutes later some other hasty worker would dash across it, carelessly slopping a basin of filthy water, medicine, or worse, all over the place?

Not that Camillus could always blame them, he thought bitterly. Most of the time they were all so rushed. The workload was merciless, and there were so few of them to

shoulder it. But he knew that at other times, their careless-
ness was on purpose. And if they dared to treat him like
that, he dreaded to think how they must treat the poor,
helpless patients. What was some dying stranger to them?
Indeed, they would make a show of kindness whenever a
doctor or supervisor was around to see, but if not, most of
the orderlies would simply ignore the pitiful summons of
the sick.

That, of course, was part of the whole problem, Camillus reflected angrily. Most of the staff were untrained men
like himself, either working here in return for medical
treatment received, or simply because no one else out
there in the crowded, bustling streets of Rome would hire
them. Suddenly, a bowl of some stinking, oozing muck
the kitchen staff had the audacity to pass off as food came
toppling down a mere foot away from Camillus, cutting off
his thoughts. He watched helplessly as it started to spread,
as if mocking him, all over the area he had just finished
scrubbing laboriously. He felt his anger rise. Enough was
enough! Some half-wit orderly was really going to regret it
this time!

He looked up savagely, searching for the culprit.

But . . . there were no other workers nearby, except for
the one who had helped him the first day. Curzio. Yes, that
was his name, Curzio Lodi. Well, it obviously hadn't been
him; he wasn't the type.

"I'm terribly sorry about that", an unsteady whisper
reached him. Camillus followed the voice until his eyes
rested on an old gentleman in a nearby bed. He was
awkwardly clutching a spoon in one withered hand, and
some of the foul-looking food had spilled down his clothes
and onto the blankets.

Camillus' anger instantly vanished. Poor old fellow! He should never have been expected to feed himself in the first place. Why, he was hardly more than a skeleton!

"Don't worry about it", Camillus assured him gently. He clambered to his feet, his leg aching from hours of kneeling on the hard floor. Who could care less about the floor anyhow? Let someone else scrub it! There were more important things to do.

"I'll help you. Wait just a moment."

Stepping over the mess, Camillus made his way to the nearby kitchen and hastily searched for a clean bowl. Two large cauldrons were simmering over the fire. He took the lid off one and peered in. It was the same revolting slop the patient had been served. Grimacing, Camillus replaced the lid and opened the other pot. A tantalizing aroma of stew wafted into the room. Camillus started to spoon some into the bowl.

The only other orderly in the kitchen looked up from the massive pile of dishes he was washing. "Hey!" he snapped. "What are you doing?"

"An old man dropped his meal. I'm bringing him another."

"Well, take it from the other pot, de Lellis! That one's for staff only!"

Camillus couldn't believe his ears. He felt himself fume. "I'll take it", he said, "from whichever pot I choose." He continued dishing up, and, just to irk the fellow, made a point of filling the bowl to the brim. Then he turned to meet the other's resentful gaze and smiled. "Care to try to stop me?"

The man hesitated, but obviously thought the better of it. A six-foot-six ex-soldier wasn't exactly the type he relished taking on. He angrily spun back around to his dishes, and Camillus, satisfied, slipped out into the ward.

It was amazing, really, how easy it was to cheer up the old gentleman. Just tell him a few stories, show him a bit of kindness; that was all it took to ease, if not his physical sufferings, at least some of his loneliness and fear. As a matter of fact, within a few minutes, the patients in the surrounding beds had turned to listen as well. Smiles broke out on their pale faces; a few shreds of laughter floated across the room.

Quietly and as unobtrusively as possible, Curzio Lodi came over and started to mop up the mess left on the floor. A pang of guilt rose in Camillus, and he got to his feet to help. But Curzio only smiled and shook his head, gesturing for Camillus to stay with the patients.

Finishing the job quickly, Curzio picked up the fragments of the broken bowl and headed into the kitchen.

At his entrance, the kitchen hand looked up and manufactured a fake smile. "Lodi!" he greeted. "Just the man I need!" He flung his dripping dishrag over Curzio's shoulder, gave him a rough slap on the back, and, with a satisfied smirk, departed from the kitchen.

Curzio peeled the wet cloth off himself and stared with dismay at the toppling stack of dishes. A sigh escaped him, but he rolled up his sleeves nonetheless and resigned himself to the unpleasant task.

The door swung open, and Camillus came in, whistling. He was obviously in better spirits. He deposited the leftover bowls he was holding onto the pile of dishes, and his eyes traveled to Curzio.

The whistling abruptly stopped.

"That's not your task", he announced.

Curzio shrugged. "It is now."

"Why that craven bully!" Camillus exploded. "You shouldn't let people treat you like that!"

Curzio averted his eyes and said nothing. Camillus realized then that he probably always let people push him around and more than likely never bothered to give it a thought. He felt his own indignation drain.

"Here," he he offered on impulse, "I'll help you." He picked up a towel. "You wash, I'll dry."

Startled, Curzio met his gaze. "You don't have to, really", he answered. "Isn't your shift just about over?"

"Isn't yours?" Camillus countered.

"I don't mind. Go and relax."

Camillus smiled wryly. "Every time I try to relax, I just end up getting into trouble."

Curzio laughed. "Well, I admit you can't get into too much trouble drying dishes."

"If there's a way, I'll find it."

Curzio's amusement proved contagious, and they both smiled. Then Curzio said with sincerity, "Thanks, Camillus."

"Don't mention it. After all, you washed my floor."

The two worked in companionable silence for a few minutes. Finally Curzio asked, "How long were you a soldier?"

"Four years, more or less. I fought my first battle when I was just under seventeen."

Curzio raised a surprised eyebrow.

"So I lied about my age", Camillus shot out defensively. Then suddenly, almost violently, he stopped working and glared at Curzio. "Look, I didn't hire myself out *just* to the Turks, you know!" he blurted out. "I've fought for plenty of Catholic princes and killed more than my fair share of Muslims as well!"

He waited to see whether or not his companion would challenge this. Curzio looked uncomfortable, but said nothing.

Relieved, Camillus picked up another wet plate and ran the towel over it. "Besides," he mumbled lamely, "I never even saw action with them. My father and I were hired as bodyguards for one of their grimy little officers. I never once raised my sword on their behalf." He had no idea why he felt compelled to justify himself to this kind, soft-spoken orderly, but for some reason he did. Maybe it was the purity and innocence in the other's eyes that unnerved him. Such innocence was something Camillus had seen but rarely in men.

There was an awkward silence, until Curzio managed to gather his courage again. "And how are you finding it here?" he asked.

"Not what I'd call thrilling."

Curzio could tell by the tone of his voice that Camillus' cheerfulness had entirely disappeared. "It takes some getting used to, but you've been here only a few days", he said encouragingly. "Give it time. Things in the hospital aren't always that bad."

Camillus cast him a miserable glance and confided, "I hope you're right."

"At least the patients seem to like you."

"You mean the ones who weren't there the other day when Moretti so considerately dragged me through the mud."

"No, I mean all of them. You treat them well, and they appreciate it."

Camillus could tell that he was being sincere and felt some of his moodiness ebb. "I like them too", he admitted, brightening a little. "What about you—why are you working in this hole?"

"I was asked to come by one of the priests who visits here sometimes. Father Neri. No doubt you'll meet him eventually. He's a good man; most people think he's a saint. He knew my family and thought this kind of work would suit me. So, well, here I am." Then changing the subject, Curzio asked, "Ever been to Rome before?"

"Only in passing."

Curzio hesitated, then offered, "If you're feeling up to it . . . I mean, if you'd like . . . maybe I can show you around a bit after we've finished cleaning up this mess."

Camillus was taken aback and wondered if his companion was motivated by pity. He glanced at Curzio suspiciously. But, no, the friendliness seemed genuine. "Sure, that'd be nice", he answered. Then he smiled and added, "And I'll even do my best to stay out of trouble for you."

IX.

Camillus could feel the doctor's sharp eyes piercing him from across the room. It was uncomfortable and annoying, but he was determined to ignore it. He looked back down at the patient in front of him and continued winding the clean bandage around the man's arm. Then he stood up, arranged the pillows as comfortably as he could, and turned to the next bed.

One of the hospital chaplains was there, an ascetic-looking middle-aged priest. He was balancing a book and a candle simultaneously in one hand, and a vessel of holy water in the other. Camillus hesitated, then decided the priest might appreciate some help. He stepped to his side and carefully took the burning candle and holy water from him.

The chaplain nodded briefly in gratitude, but didn't interrupt the flow of his prayer, ". . . *intercessione, a praesenti liberari tristitia, et aeterna perfrui laetitia. Per Christum Dominum nostrum.*"

Camillus sensed he was waiting for him to say something. He glanced at the priest with uncertainty and mumbled the only answer he could think of. "Amen."

To his relief, it was the correct response. The priest seemed satisfied and closed his book. Then, raising his hand over the patient, he imparted the blessing of Almighty God. *"Benedictio Dei omnipotentis, Patris et Filii et Spiritus Sancti, descendat super te, et maneat semper."*

"Amen", Camillus repeated with slightly more confidence this time. He too made the sign of the cross, upon himself, and blew out the candle.

The chaplain took the sick man's hand and assured him, "I'll come again tomorrow, I promise."

The patient smiled and nodded.

Stepping away a few paces, the priest motioned for Camillus to join him. "He may need me during the night", he confided in a low voice. "Could I ask you to send for me if he gets worse?"

Camillus' shift was ending within the hour, but he made a quick decision not to let the priest know that. The patient was obviously dying; he might not survive until the morning. "I'll stay with him myself tonight, Father, if you'd like", Camillus offered. He knew in his heart that he couldn't leave the poor man alone and afraid in his trying hours. Perhaps he had a son somewhere, a son who didn't even know his father was dying and couldn't be there with him.

"That's very good of you. Thank you, my boy", the priest said. Then, extending his hand, he warmly introduced himself, "I'm Father Philip Neri. Don't tell me—Camillus de Lellis, yes?"

The two shook hands, and Camillus regarded him with suspicion. But the priest cheerfully explained his source of knowledge. "I've heard quite a bit about you from the patients here. You seem to have won their hearts these last few weeks."

The unexpected compliment astonished Camillus. He looked confused for a moment, then admitted, "I like it here." His own words, however, made him grimace, and he added candidly, "I never thought I would say that!"

The priest looked at him encouragingly, and Camillus lowered his guard a little. "It's good to be helping somehow. Most of these men are far worse off than I am, and so", he shrugged, "I just try to cheer them up."

Father Neri patted him on the shoulder. "Keep it up, my son. You're doing more good in this hospital than you realize."

Camillus stole a glance across the room and couldn't keep the bitterness out of his voice. "Doctor Moretti doesn't think so."

The priest raised an eyebrow. "Doctor Moretti? Don't let him worry you. He runs his wards like an army camp—"

"Worse!"

"—but he's a good man, and an excellent doctor. He'd lay down his life for any one of his patients. Oh, I admit, he's stubborn and hot-headed, yes . . ." he smiled with amusement, "but so, they tell me, are you!"

Camillus opened his mouth to defend himself, but the twinkle in the priest's eye warned him the man was no fool. Instead he changed his mind and admitted, "I'm . . . um . . . working on that, Father."

Now Father Neri's face broke into a genuine smile. "Good, good! Continue to work, as hard as you can. That's all the good God asks of you. You must learn, Camillus, to *surrender* . . ." He quickly raised his hand to forestall the coming objection, and continued, "I know, I know! Not a word a soldier likes to hear! Nevertheless, surrender you must—to Almighty God. His grace will do the rest."

Camillus was looking hard at the priest, the words starting to sink in. At least partially. "Thanks, Father. I'll try to remember that", he promised.

The two men smiled at each other, then Camillus turned and went back to begin his long and lonely vigil at the dying patient's side.

X.

Curzio emerged from the church into the darkness and, although the night was mild, instinctively pulled his cloak a bit more tightly around him. It was late, very late in fact, and he felt the vague uneasiness that any reasonable man would feel, alone and unarmed, in this area of Rome. He wondered with regret if perhaps he shouldn't have stayed in the chapel quite so long. But the time had passed quickly.

He was halfway down the steps when he spotted the

drunken, laughing band of men swaggering into the street from the alley. Cautiously, Curzio stood still and waited, certain, at least, that they hadn't seen him. Yet.

The men had come from the direction of the docks, he realized without surprise. The docks of the Tiber River were infamous for their rough, shady gambling dens and the villainous sailors who frequented them. The very dregs of Roman humanity, as far as Curzio was concerned! He watched as the little group stopped at the corner. A few of them tilted their flasks back and drained the contents. Then they all bid each other a noisy, boisterous farewell and dispersed in different directions.

Curzio took a few more hesitant steps, his eyes and ears still alert for danger. Only one of the scoundrels remained in sight now, heading, unfortunately, in the same direction Curzio needed to go. Well, there was nothing he could do about it. Besides, the man was far enough behind him that Curzio figured he could get a substantial head start if he really tried. He stepped out onto the street and started walking as fast as he could.

"Hey! Wait up!"

Curzio's blood almost froze. For an instant he wondered if he should make a dash for it, but decided that might only provoke the thug more. Instead he quickened his stride and refused to turn around.

"I said, wait!"

His mind raced. Was the man armed? Could he fight him? Or should he simply run?

"Curzio!"

He was calling him by name! Who of that rough bunch could possibly know who he was? Bewildered, Curzio spun around, his muscles tensing.

"Something wrong with you? Didn't you hear me the first time?"

A flood of relief washed over him as he recognized Camillus trying to catch up. But his relief soon gave way to dismay as the pungent smell of alcohol reached him, and he realized his friend's speech was slurred.

Completely unaware of Curzio's pounding heart and slightly damp palms, Camillus asked brightly, "So, what nocturnal adventures bring you out to these parts?"

Curzio watched as his drunken friend stumbled into step beside him and quietly replied, "Maybe I should ask you the same question."

"Me?" Camillus grinned. "Just felt the urge to boost the financial situation somewhat, if you get my meaning. Those hospital wages leave something to be desired, don't you find?"

Inwardly Curzio groaned, but decided to refrain from comment. The two started walking back to the hospital together, albeit one of them unsteadily. Camillus, however, sensed the other's disapproval and gave him a lighthearted punch on the arm. "Oh, come now, Curzio!" he said, "It was only a bit of harmless fun."

Over the past weeks the unlikely pair had become fast friends. Entirely opposite though they were, the two had formed an inexplicable liking for one another.

Now Curzio cast his friend a reproachful glance and warned gravely, "You shouldn't go around with company like that, Camillus. Don't you know they could teach you all sorts of bad habits?"

"*Them?*" Camillus laughed. "They couldn't teach me one solitary, isolated little thing!" He opened his cloak and proudly showed Curzio the heavy bag of money concealed therein. With a conceited grin, he continued, "On the contrary, my friend, in point of fact, the whole lot of 'em received what you might call an advanced lesson in—" But at Curzio's stern look, Camillus decided not to finish his sentence.

Curzio cleared his throat and admonished softly, "Those sailors are nothing but a bunch of low-down, cutthroat ruffians. Really, Camillus, you can't be safe with them."

Camillus tried hard to keep a straight face this time and replied solemnly, "You're right, Curzio. Nasty company." He shook his head. "Downright nasty!"

"It's not funny!" Curzio persisted, but realized with exasperation that Camillus found it hilarious. Suddenly he stopped walking and put a restraining hand on Camillus' arm. "What was that noise?" he asked.

They both halted, listening.

"I dunno," Camillus answered, unconcerned.

They stood there another minute, waiting, before Camillus finally shrugged and said, "Don't worry about it." He moved on and Curzio joined him.

But the unfamiliar noise started up again, and the two looked at each other with growing curiosity. It almost sounded like . . . but surely not at this hour . . .

"Someone is crying, I think. A child, maybe?" Curzio volunteered.

"You may be right."

"Perhaps someone's lost. Or hurt. We'd better go and see." Without waiting for a reply, Curzio headed off in the direction of the sound. Indifferently, Camillus went after him.

Sure enough, a little girl, filthy, thin, and ragged, was sitting alone on a doorstep down a dark alley, her body racked with sobs. She glanced up at the men's approach, but she was too young to register any fear. Instead, she wiped her eyes with the back of her hand and looked up at them.

"Are you here to help?" she asked with innocent trust.

Camillus glanced at his friend. He was out of his depth here and hoped Curzio would know what to say. To his great relief, Curzio crouched down in front of the child and answered gently, "We'll help if we can. Tell us what's wrong."

"It's Mama! See, she's so sick! And now all the others have it too! Except, of course, Ricardo. He never gets sick. He's still all right, but . . . but . . . we've run out of food now, and . . . and . . ."

"Show us where they are", Curzio instructed.

The little girl popped up, visibly brightening. She eagerly grabbed Curzio's cloak, pulling him into the dark, forbidding building. Helplessly, Camillus followed.

Down this dim hall, then that, up one flight of rickety old stairs, then another, the child led the way. At last she pushed open a door, and the three were struck by the sickening odor of disease and filth.

The two orderlies were faced with what they were dreading the most—a roomful of wailing, sick children and an even sicker mother lying upon the sagging cot against the wall.

She opened her sunken eyes and instantly recoiled with terror at the sight of the two strange men standing inside her doorway, one of average build, but the other quite a bit bigger. Her hand flew to her mouth as if to scream, but no sound would come.

"We won't hurt you, I promise!" Curzio assured her quickly.

But she didn't look in the least bit convinced.

"They came to help, Mama", her daughter said happily, but the innocent words did nothing to calm the frightened mother.

From the corner of the room someone stood up and protectively moved toward the bed. To their relief, the two men saw it was a teenage boy. Well, this would at least make things a bit easier.

"We work at San Giacomo Hospital", Curzio explained. "Honestly, we're not going to hurt you." He hoped that the overpowering stench in the room would hide the smell of alcohol still pervading his companion.

The woman nodded, but continued to stare with apprehension.

"Uh . . . where's your husband?" Camillus asked.

It was the wrong thing to say. The woman shrank back in fear, obviously unwilling to tell them.

"Mama doesn't know", the teenage boy answered bitterly. "He left about a year ago. I'm Ricardo."

The two orderlies looked around the room with despair. It was obvious that the whole place would need washing and disinfecting, a fire would have to be lit to heat water, these people would all somehow need to be cleaned and fed, and . . . and . . . the list was endless. Camillus pulled Curzio aside and whispered, "Should we try and get them all to the hospital?"

Curzio shook his head. "How? I doubt very much the woman's going to let us simply pick them up and whisk them away! Besides, that place would scare these little ones half to death."

Camillus nodded in agreement and gave a tipsy smile. "Well, then, as the saying goes," he began sagely, "if the horse refuses to walk to the lake, then simply let the lake walk to the horse." He knit his brows in deep concentration and pondered gravely, "Or was it a cow?"

Curzio grimaced, deciding no answer was merited. "Look, we'll need to find a woman—don't ask me where!—to help out here", he whispered back in his most reasonable tone of voice, hoping he was getting through. But somehow doubting that he was. "Unless, of course, bathing babies is one of your hidden specialties?"

Camillus grinned. "I've done a lot of things in my day, Curzio, but I can't honestly boast of any broad expertise in that area."

"That makes two of us. As I said, we need to find a female somewhere." He turned to the boy and asked, "Ricardo, do you know any woman around here? I mean someone who could get all these children and your mother washed up while we go back to the hospital for a few supplies?"

Ricardo reflected. "There's only Signora Vian across the hall. But she won't dare come in here. She's too afraid she'll catch it."

The two friends glanced at each other with dismay.

Camillus narrowed his eyes and tried hard to think. It wasn't easy, this thinking business, at the end of all those empty flagons, but he tried his best. Finally an idea came to him and he reached into his cloak and pulled out a few dazzling gold coins. The boy's eyes widened, and Camillus asked, "Think she'd overcome her fears at the sight of these?"

In a flash, Ricardo was out the door with the money to find out.

"Now, listen," Curzio began, "I'm going to start by

airing out the place." He studied Camillus with concern. "Could I trust you to light a fire without burning down the building?" he asked.

"A fire? Absolutely. No problem." But the dazed look on Camillus' face warned Curzio that it might actually be a problem. Camillus ran a hand through his hair and cast his friend a sheepish look. "Uh . . . just give me a moment to remember what's involved. I'm sure it'll come back."

He looked so pathetic that it required all Curzio's self-control not to burst out laughing.

Or, alternatively, to turn around and hit him!

But, in the end, he did neither. He just shook his head and requested, "Do me a favor, Camillus. Keep your distance from the poor woman and try not to say anything. She is far too petrified of you as it is."

He realized, to his profound satisfaction, that Camillus actually looked embarrassed.

No, definitely no point in hitting him, Curzio decided. The alcohol would hit him hard enough by morning anyhow.

By the time Ricardo returned with a sleepy-eyed, but miraculously eager, Signora Vian, the windows had been forced open after many years of disuse, and a warm fire was starting to crackle. The presence of another woman calmed the mother, and she finally closed her eyes and seemed to relax.

"We're going back to the hospital for food, blankets, and medicine", Curzio told Signora Vian. "While we're gone, you start heating some water and giving baths."

Camillus glared at her and warned, "And those are some pretty expensive baths you'll be giving, signora, so you'd better do a good job or else!"

Curzio grinned. "I'd follow his advice if I were you. Believe me, you don't want to incur my friend's wrath." With that, he took Camillus by the arm and steered him out of the small apartment.

The two men had more than one trip to the hospital to make, and several hours' hard work ahead of them. But the end result was not only a sparkling clean room and comfortable, fed patients, but also the return of sobriety for one of the workers. As the first rays of sunlight filtered through the narrow windows, the exhausted pair knew they had done all they could.

"We'll tell Father Neri about you the next time we see him. He'll know what else to do to help", Curzio promised the now weakly smiling mother. He gathered up the few remaining supplies and headed toward the door.

But Camillus motioned for him to wait. Then, trying hard to ignore his aching head and delicate stomach, he called Ricardo over to the table and poured out a pile of shining coins from his leather pouch. "As soon as the market opens, go and buy more food", he instructed the astonished boy. "And new clothes. And, well, whatever else your mother says." He paused, considering, then finally muttered, "Oh, why not?" as he tossed the entire pouch onto the table. Then he gave the stupefied lad a friendly slap on the back and joined Curzio at the door.

As the two stepped out onto the street, Curzio could recognize the aftereffects of his friend's heavy drinking of the night before. He couldn't resist a dig. "So, how are you feeling?" he asked, keeping his voice casual.

Camillus groaned. "Absolutely revolting", he admitted with honesty. But then he cast Curzio a suspicious look.

"That's exactly what you wanted to hear, wasn't it?" he blurted out with amazement. "I can see it gives you immense satisfaction!"

Curzio tried hard to keep a straight face. He snapped his fingers and announced in his most innocent voice, "Oh, must've slipped my mind! I meant to tell you: you've got the early morning shift today." At the look of utter despair on Camillus' face, however, he could no longer refrain from laughing. "And you've been assigned to assist Doctor Moretti on his rounds!"

Curzio dodged just in time to avoid the bottle of medicine flung at him and easily outsprinted Camillus.

But he'd already known for hours that he'd cover up for his friend. There was still enough time to swap their names on the hospital roster, and Doctor Moretti would be none the wiser.

XI.

The low-burning lamps cast flickering shadows across the walls. The room was quiet at this hour of the night, most of the patients having finally succumbed to their restless sleep. Curzio sat drowsily at the table in the corner, trying to keep himself awake by rolling the laundered bandages into tidy bundles.

Someone entered the ward, but he didn't bother to look up. The sound of the opening cupboard told him it was just another orderly, on night duty elsewhere, searching for extra medical supplies.

After a moment, however, the newcomer slumped down into a nearby chair, and Curzio glanced up from his task with mild curiosity. Aghast, he bolted upright and stared at the other as the cloth held against his face was rapidly turning a dark crimson.

"What on earth happened to you?" Curzio demanded, rising to his feet.

Camillus gingerly lowered the cloth a fraction and looked at him with dazed eyes. "Nothing."

"What do you mean—nothing? Let me see it!"

"I said it's nothing!" Camillus insisted, stubbornly pushing his friend's hand away.

"And *I* said, let me see it!"

Camillus relented and obediently let the cloth drop. "How could I know the rotten devil had a dagger up his sleeve?" he mumbled lamely as his friend let out a low whistle.

Curzio hurried over to the cupboard and returned with a handful of supplies, which he dumped onto the table. Then he quickly soaked a piece of linen and started to clean the gushing wound.

"Hey!" Camillus flinched.

"Sorry, Camillus. I have to", Curzio apologized. Then he added candidly, "I'm glad I'm not standing in the shoes of whoever it was that did this."

"Not even he is standing in his own shoes right now. And probably won't be for a while."

A ghost of a smile passed over Curzio's face. Indeed, he had no trouble believing that. "Are you going to tell me what happened?" he asked.

Camillus shrugged, almost with indifference. After a moment, however, he wearily answered, "I saw another worker attacking one of the patients. The poor fellow just asked him for a drink of water, and the brute flew into a rage. . . . Threw the man off his bed and started beating him."

Curzio froze for an instant in disbelief. But, no, he knew his friend was telling the truth. He'd witnessed similar acts of violence himself in the past. He cleared his throat and announced steadily, "This needs stitches."

"Go ahead."

"You know I'm not a doctor."

"You should see some of the fine little operations I've performed on friends in the battlefield."

"Come on, Camillus. This is a hospital, not a battlefield. There are plenty of doctors who—"

"Who all think I'm scum!" Camillus interrupted bitterly.

"That's not true!"

But to Curzio's dismay, Camillus rose to his feet and declared angrily, "Then forget it! I'll do it myself!"

With a sigh, Curzio gently pushed him back down. "No, you won't", he gave in.

"This place is despicable!" Camillus suddenly exploded with vehemence. "The patients are neglected—abused even!—left rotting in their own filth! And no one lifts a finger to help them!"

"You do", Curzio answered calmly. "And I do. Now, just be quiet and stay still."

"And they call this the best hospital in Rome!"

"Apparently it is. Would you please stay still?"

"You'll never believe what I saw the other day!"

"Oh yes I would", Curzio said, a faint trace of exasperation creeping into his voice.

"A patient was so thirsty that he started drinking a bottle of medicine some stupid orderly left lying around—"

"*Camillus!* Do you want me to do this or not?"

"Sorry", Camillus said with instant contrition. He

clamped his mouth shut and closed his eyes, grateful that the adrenaline rising from anger was still pumping through him. Adrenaline, he had found over the years, was something of a painkiller.

"I've seen worse in my day", Curzio admitted quietly after a few minutes of concentration. "Some of them have been known to drink the oil from their lamps."

Camillus winced, whether from disgust, or pain, or a combination of both, Curzio couldn't be sure.

Unbidden images sharply invaded Camillus' memory— starving soldiers desperately carving out the livers from dead comrades after some bloody skirmish; others going insane with thirst during those long and ruthless sieges in the Moorish desert wastes. He tried to force the memories away.

But they wouldn't depart.

"There are so many people suffering in the world", he finally said with an effort, his anger draining. "And no one cares about them." He opened his eyes and looked at his friend, his expression so genuinely imploring that Curzio hadn't the heart to cut him off again.

"It's not that no one cares, Camillus. It's just that there's no solution to the problem. I'm afraid hospitals like this are all there are."

"But they're not good enough. We both know they're just not good enough!" Camillus objected. "There has to be a better answer than that!"

"I wish there were", Curzio said. "But there isn't. At least not as far as I can see. Unless someone finds a way to revolutionize the entire hospital system. Staff them with dedicated workers who truly devote themselves to the care of the patients. But don't ask me how. Most of the men who work in places like this are only here for the money. You know that as well as I do." Curzio shook his head helplessly. "Just try to hold still another minute—I'm nearly done with this."

He finished patching up the wound and apologized: "I don't think it would exactly earn me a doctor's degree, but it's the best I can do. Sorry."

"Thanks, Curzio", Camillus said. "I'm indebted to you."

"Are you hurt anywhere else?"

"No. I'm all right."

"Are you sure?"

"Yes."

Curzio sat down on the edge of the table, and the two friends looked at each other, both disheartened by the hopelessness of it all.

"Do you know what bothers me the most?" Curzio confided after a moment. "All the people in poverty. Who takes care of them when they're sick or dying?"

They both knew the answer.

"What can we do to help them?" Camillus persisted.

"That's the problem! Don't you see? There is nothing we can do."

"But there has to be something, Curzio! Of course we can't take away all the sufferings on the face of the earth, but at least we can lessen some of them."

Curzio shrugged, entirely at a loss. "Well, maybe you're right. But if there is something we can do, then it's beyond me to imagine what it might be." He smiled sadly and added, "But if you really think you can come up with an answer, Camillus, then go ahead. And believe me, I'll be the first to support you."

XII.

It was always a comfort to be with his own kind again, Camillus thought to himself as he wheeled the meal trolley down the corridor. He usually saved this next room for last, simply because it was nice to end the day's duties on a good note. Somehow the company of other soldiers cheered him up. They were in the same situation as he, and all shared that same helpless frustration of being confined in this rotten hospital for month after endless month.

But on this particular day, Camillus had a little detour to make before bringing the men their evening meal. He cast a cautious glance up and down the hall. All looked safe; no one was in sight. He steered the trolley into a nearby supply room and located the small barrel he had hidden in the corner. Pulling off the blanket concealing it, Camillus quickly lifted the keg onto the trolley and draped a towel over it. Then he headed back out into the corridor and continued on his way.

There were only a handful of patients in the small room, all soldiers wounded in combat and fortunate enough to have been transported to a hospital by their comrades. Camillus firmly closed the door behind him, and his unexpected action caused the men to look up with mild curiosity. But at his conspiratorial wink, they readily fell in with their orderly's mood.

With a flourish, Camillus unveiled the keg, and, as the others watched in astonishment, he commented with feigned surprise, "Well, what do y'know! This certainly looks like an interesting pot of soup! I wonder who could have planned today's menu?"

Instantly cheers of amusement and pleasure broke out

among the soldiers, and they eagerly pulled themselves into sitting positions on their beds.

"I just thought it appropriate to celebrate the great Catholic victory against the Turks at Lepanto we've all been hearing so much about", Camillus explained with a grin. Then he served up the beverage the only way he could think of . . . by dipping the soup bowls into the keg and passing them out. But the men didn't seem to mind the unusual drinking vessels; they were only too grateful he'd managed to smuggle the stuff into the hospital at all.

They waited patiently until all had received their treat, Camillus himself included, then, of one accord, lifted their bowls into the air for a toast.

"To our brave comrades at Lepanto!" one of them proposed with gusto.

"And to those of us who should've been there fighting with them", Camillus added feelingly.

The soldiers all nodded in solemn, and somewhat poignant, agreement and drank. Then Camillus busied himself serving up the food while the others sat back in contentment and enjoyed the first real drink they'd had since their entrance to San Giacomo.

It worked like magic. Within minutes the men were laughing and swapping stories of past adventures.

They needed moments like these, Camillus reflected to himself, to keep up their morale. They all did, he himself perhaps more than any of them. Every man in this room longed to return to the old familiar army camps, the gambling and drinking and reckless ways that were all they'd ever known and all they lived for.

Their laughter and merrymaking increased in volume, but Camillus didn't mind. It was good to see them so cheerful and lively for once. He continued passing out the meals, and refilling their bowls as the need arose, which didn't take long.

It was only when the noise came to an abrupt end, and a few of the men shot him warning glances that Camillus realized someone had entered the room. He spun back to the trolley and quickly draped a cover over the keg, but knew with a sinking heart that he hadn't been fast enough.

Just as he'd dreaded, the doctor's sharp eyes had already spotted it.

An awkward hush fell upon the room. None of the patients quite knew what to do to rescue their poor orderly. They realized, as well as he, that no doctor ever came in at this hour. The intrusion had come as a complete surprise. The men could only exchange worried glances and hope for the best.

Moretti strode forward and whipped the towel off the trolley. He regarded first the contraband, then his employee, with equal disgust. Finally, clearing his throat, he demanded, "Need I ask what *this* is doing in my ward!"

Camillus opened his mouth to say something, but the doctor gave him no chance.

"How dare you—*how dare you!*—introduce my patients to such . . . such base goings-on!"

One of the other men jumped in. "Aw, Doc! It weren't no introduction! Us an' the booze are old friends."

A few of the others sniggered, but instantly relapsed into silence at Moretti's piercing look.

Camillus felt his own temper rising. "Doctor Moretti, these men are wounded, not sick! A little wine can't do them any harm!"

Moretti raised a skeptical eyebrow and took a whiff of

the contents of the keg. "Wine?" he mocked. "Wine, did you say? What do you take me for, de Lellis? A complete fool?"

Another soldier piped up. "Now, now, Doctor. He was only trying to brighten things up a little!"

But Camillus had no intention of backing down this time. "You can't treat these patients like children!" he returned hotly. "They're grown, responsible men, and—"

"Just as well, de Lellis, as you yourself obviously are not! Therefore I have no choice but to—"

Camillus, however, didn't wait for the doctor to finish his sentence. Instead he shoved past him and stormed out the door, making very certain it slammed hard behind him.

The soldiers all glared at Moretti resentfully and sank back down onto their beds.

"Don't be too hard on him, Doc", the oldest among them finally said. "He's still just a boy."

"He's also one of the most dedicated nurses you've got around here, and you know it!" another added.

"Besides," warned a third, "Father Neri has taken quite a liking to that young man."

* * *

Camillus stalked into the staff refectory and, angrily grabbing a chair, slumped down in embittered silence.

The other orderlies at the table didn't bother even glancing up from their meals. They had become used to his sharp mood swings and weren't particularly interested. Curzio alone stopped eating and looked at his friend, waiting for some explanation. When none was forthcoming, he offered, "There's still plenty of food, Camillus. Want anything?"

Camillus looked up with a slightly dazed expression, as

if it had only just dawned on him that he wasn't alone in the room. Gloomily he shook his head and looked away again.

Curzio had learned by experience not to pry. Especially when his friend was in a foul mood. He finished his own meal and left to put his plate away.

Camillus instinctively waited till he was gone, then, not even caring what the others might think, reached into his jacket and pulled out a small flask hidden in its depths. He took a long swig, undaunted by the fact that all the men at the table were eyeing him with a mixture of surprise and envy. They obviously decided, however, that it was best not to comment.

The drink seemed to brighten his dismal mood a little, and Camillus sat up straighter as a sudden inspiration came to him. Reaching into one of his boots, he produced a deck of cards and started to shuffle them on the table invitingly.

"Anyone for a hand or two?" he tempted with a cocky smile.

Every man at the table froze, attention riveted hungrily on the deck.

"Haven't even *seen* a pack of those things since I started working in this hole!" a wistful voice broke through the ensuing silence.

Immediately there was a general murmur of agreement, although no one made a move to get closer.

"Well?" Camillus encouraged.

Torn between their strong desire and their common sense, no one quite dared volunteer.

To Camillus' dismay, Curzio unexpectedly returned to the table, unaware of what was going on. But he instantly spotted the flask and the deck of cards. He stiffened and shot a warning look at his friend. Camillus quickly averted his eyes, and Curzio could tell without a doubt that he was feeling a distinct pang of guilt.

"Camillus, don't", Curzio ventured to admonish softly. "You know the rules."

The other men had already started to waver. A few pushed their unfinished food aside and scraped their chairs closer with pathetic indecision.

"Camillus," Curzio repeated, "don't do it! What if you're caught?"

Still refusing to meet his eyes, Camillus merely shrugged and said, "No one will care. We're off duty." For the first time, he found himself annoyed by his pious friend's presence. He wished Curzio hadn't seen. But he stubbornly decided to ignore him and looked directly at the others instead. "Are you nothing but a bunch of old ladies?" he provoked.

Still they hesitated.

Rolling his eyes, Camillus dug into his pouch and tossed a handful of coins on the table. "All right, look", he said with his most disarming smile, "I'll even make it a bit more attractive for you."

XIII.

There was ice between those two, Curzio thought. Frozen, immovable ice.

It was so tangible that he almost shuddered with cold. How the other orderlies in the dormitory weren't affected by it, he couldn't understand. But then again, what did they care?

He stole another glance toward the bed. Doctor Moretti was examining the wound on Camillus' leg, displeasure and frustration stamped all over his face. Camillus refused so much as even to look at him. His eyes were hard and defiant, but Curzio could tell that the pain was intense. Neither spoke to the other.

It was getting worse again. Curzio didn't have to be a doctor to see that. The mysterious wound had even Moretti baffled. Sometimes it would respond to treatment for a while, but then the infection would flare up again for no apparent reason.

The doctor wrapped a fresh bandage around it and stood up. He looked at his patient as if about to say something, but Camillus stubbornly turned his face away.

Yes, definitely, ice. That was the only word Curzio could think of.

Moretti shrugged with irritation and briskly strode from the room.

The few other orderlies had already started to depart toward the refectory. Curzio went over to the bed and asked, "Are you coming?"

"No", Camillus answered, brooding.

"Then would you like me to bring a meal in here for you?"

"No. I'm not hungry."

Curzio sighed. "Look, Camillus, I know it hurts, but you still need to eat once in a while. You can't survive solely off the contents of your little flask."

Camillus looked at him coldly. "And when were you appointed my dietician? I've got enough caring doctors watching over me like hawks."

"If the administration is always on your back, it's only because you've put them there."

"Just for once, Curzio, leave me alone. I'm not feeling very friendly right now. And you can take that as a warning!"

"Wake up, Camillus. How long do you think it's going to be before the authorities discover what's been taking place behind their backs?"

"I said, leave me alone."

"How long before someone accidentally stumbles onto one of your secret card games in the supply room, or finds the stash of—"

"Must I tell you a third time!"

Curzio shut his mouth. He looked around the room. They were the only two left. If only Camillus would cooperate with him, he thought to himself. He was always so bitter these days! Pain was one thing, yes. And Curzio had all the compassion in the world for him. But that wasn't the only problem. Camillus just wasn't trying anymore. At all! He was acting like an irascible, hard-headed mule these past several weeks, and that was all there was to it.

Curzio forced himself to speak calmly. "I know the pain must be hard to bear, but your leg will heal eventually. It has to! You won't be here forever."

Camillus shook his head, discouraged. "It's been nearly nine months, Curzio. Just how long does it take a so-called doctor to—"

"He's doing the best he can!"

Camillus relented. "I know", he admitted grudgingly. "It's not his fault." He stood up and painfully made a move toward his cloak.

Curzio would have reached out to give him a hand, but he knew instinctively that Camillus wouldn't appreciate it just then. Instead he said quietly, "I don't think it's that cold in the refectory."

"I'm not going to the refectory."

"Oh. I see." Curzio couldn't hide the edge of sarcasm in his voice. He felt so helpless. "The docks again, is it? Maybe that's where you've been taking all your meals lately. Heaven knows you spend enough time there these days."

Camillus shot him a chilly look.

Curzio knew it wasn't the right time to persist in this conversation. But there was never a right time anymore. Camillus was always like this now. So different from how he used to be.

"Those sailors really aren't the best company you could choose, Camillus. You know it yourself."

To his surprise, Camillus gave a hollow laugh. "Just how ignorant can you be, Curzio?" he asked with amazement. "I'm no better than any of them! Haven't you realized that much by now, after all these months?"

"Oh, yes, you are!" Curzio answered. "That is, you could be. If you wanted to."

Camillus shrugged with indifference. But his voice softened. "You're a loyal friend, Curzio. You really are. But you're a hopelessly blind one as well."

"I'm not as blind and ignorant as you seem to think! As a matter of fact, I can see things a lot more clearly than you can lately."

Camillus sighed.

Curzio could recognize those signs of increasing ill temper and knew it was taking an effort for his friend to control them. He sensed it would be wise to tread more carefully, but he himself was getting fed up. "I'm only trying to help you", he said, starting to lose his patience.

Unexpectedly, Camillus exploded. "Well, save your

breath! It's something you can't understand!" He swept his arm around the room and angrily declared, "I wasn't born for *this*! I'm a soldier, not a servant! I just want to get on with my life again! I miss the army, I miss the fighting—"

"Well, there's plenty of fighting for you right here! Start by conquering yourself!" Curzio blurted out, the anger in his own voice startling him.

Camillus froze, stunned.

Curzio knew he should just stop now, but somehow he couldn't. He felt his own ire mounting quickly. Far too quickly. It was something he wasn't used to and had little experience controlling.

"You think you know so much about courage, Camillus? Well, the truth is, courage comes in a lot of different forms . . . and God is interested in only one of them! You're not a soldier; you're not even a servant! You're nothing but a *slave*, Camillus! A slave to your own self-will!"

It was too late. The words were out.

Camillus was staring at him with an expression Curzio had never seen before, but sensed meant danger. He suddenly felt his heart start to pound more rapidly and knew he had gone too far. He had never intended the words to be so brutal. They had just come tumbling out before he had had a chance to think, and he instantly regretted them.

"I'm sorry, Camillus", he got out with an effort. "I didn't mean—"

"I think you did!"

His eyes. Something about the look in his eyes made Curzio take a step back, his muscles tensing in sudden fear. He had a fleeting memory of that other orderly, the one with the dagger who had started to beat a patient that night, and how he had looked when Camillus was done with him. The thought was anything but comforting.

Nonetheless, summoning every ounce of his own courage, Curzio continued as steadily as he could, "You have it in you to rise above yourself, Camillus. I know you do! And it's not even a battle you have to fight alone. God will help you—*He wants to help you!* But He can't unless you let Him!"

The two locked eyes for a long, challenging minute, both unwilling to back down.

Finally Camillus, unwilling to hurt his defenseless friend and knowing deep in his heart that he himself was the weaker, could do nothing but feign contempt and haughty indifference. With a smirk of disgust, he flung on his cloak and abruptly left the room.

Curzio hadn't realized he had been holding his breath until he let it out. Trembling, he sank back onto the edge of the bed, fighting to control his badly shaken nerves. He had only wanted to help, to raise Camillus' fighting blood in the right direction. But he suspected, with a sinking heart, that he had succeeded only in pushing his friend further the other way.

He felt drained all of a sudden, as if he himself had just been in a battle. He forced himself to his feet again and grabbed his own cloak. Well, at least there was One to Whom he could pour out his heart. One Who would always be willing to help.

XIV.

Curzio found he had lost track of the time . . . again! That seemed to have become a problem for him lately, ever since that terrible confrontation he had had with Camillus last week in the dormitory. He just wasn't thinking straight anymore. Too busy brooding about it all the time.

But now he realized that he had better return to the hospital. Darkness had fallen, and the shadows were lengthening rapidly around him. He knew he really shouldn't be out in these parts at this hour. He had thought a walk might help him sort things out, but perhaps it hadn't been such a good idea to go quite this far. In the stillness, he could hear the riotous shouts and laughter from the nearby docks, and it only depressed him more. He tried hard not to imagine Camillus being part of it, but in vain. He knew he was there. He always was!

If only Camillus would give him a chance to apologize, Curzio thought with a heavy heart. He hadn't planned for that conversation to get so out of hand. Not that he could really reproach himself for what he had said. After all, it was true. But he never should have lost his own temper and wounded his friend's pride like that. No, that had been entirely the wrong approach to take with Camillus. It had only raised his hackles, and understandably so! Every time Curzio recalled the words, he wanted to kick himself. Why hadn't he remained calm? Or better still, why hadn't he waited for a better moment to broach the subject at all? He had known Camillus was in a foul mood; indeed, Camillus had warned him more than once to back off and leave him alone. So why hadn't he listened?

Curzio sighed. What chance did he stand now of putting things right between them? Camillus hadn't once deigned to look at him, much less speak to him, in the past week. No, there had only been that hurtful, stony silence every time Curzio went anywhere near him. What hope was there of ever getting through that cold, hard barrier now?

A sudden noise somewhere behind him drew Curzio out of his thoughts. Instinctively, he spun around and strained his eyes to see through the darkness.

He could see no one there. The narrow alleyway looked deserted.

A bit too deserted in fact.

Curzio felt a chill run up his spine. Those shadows over there. Was that a movement? Or was it just his imagination? He wasn't sure.

He turned back around and quickened his stride.

* * *

Camillus simply couldn't concentrate on the game. He'd been trying—he really had—but it just wasn't working this time. He had lost every hand he had played, and not even the liquor was cheering him up tonight. As a matter of fact, he wasn't in the mood to drink at all. The drunken cheerfulness of the others in the tavern only served to irk him.

Why did Curzio's words have to keep invading his mind, creeping in to spoil every potentially enjoyable evening this week? Why did he even care so much what Curzio thought?

But he *did* care! That was the problem.

Dismally, Camillus chucked in his cards and stood up. He mumbled a lame excuse to his companions, paid for his untouched drink, and miserably left the tavern.

* * *

Curzio felt his apprehension increasing by the minute. He stole another glance over his shoulder, but all that met his eyes was the same shadowy blackness. Still, he couldn't shake off the uncanny sensation of being followed.

It was all in his mind, he reassured himself with annoyance. Of course there was nobody lurking back there.

He heard another noise. Much closer. Something banging, then what sounded like muffled voices.

He forced himself to stay calm and wondered what he could use as a weapon. What on earth had he been thinking to have wandered out into these hostile slums? How stupid could he have been?

There was a church up ahead. He spotted the towering facade looming in the dark. If he could make it there, then maybe, just maybe, a few people would still be inside. Doubtful at this time of night, of course, but it was his best chance.

Instinctively Curzio broke into a run.

So also, as he clearly heard now, did several pairs of footsteps behind him.

* * *

Camillus sullenly made his way through the maze of alleys toward the hospital. He was in no hurry to get back. There was no privacy there, nowhere to be alone to think. The other orderlies in the dormitory only irritated him.

And then, of course, there was the perpetual problem of trying to avoid Curzio these days. He was probably asleep, yes . . . but what if he weren't? Camillus didn't want to be seen coming in, didn't want him to know he'd been at the docks again.

But, of course, Curzio knew. He wasn't stupid.

The hurtful words came to Camillus' mind again. They cut through him keenly. What right had Curzio to fling such insults? A slave! How dare he!

Yet deep inside Camillus knew the accusation was true! He felt his depression increase. Yes, that was what made it so hard to take: everything Curzio had thrown at him was true! He was a slave to his passions!

He sighed. If only there were someone he could confide in. Someone to unburden his heart to. But who could possibly care about him with all his faults and failures?

The dim outline of a distant church caught his eye. The Blessed Sacrament was there. The God about Whom Father Neri so often spoke with such encouragement. Hidden in the tabernacle. Waiting. Always waiting.

On impulse, Camillus suddenly decided where to go.

* * *

Even as Curzio was dashing up the steps, he could see the door was closed against him. He should have known! Of course the church would be locked at this hour!

But there was nowhere else to go! His pursuers were right behind him, practically on his heels.

He whirled around, knowing with dreadful certainty that he was trapped. Would they let him go once they realized he had no money? Before he could even think what to do, he felt an agonizing blow to his stomach and doubled over, suddenly unable to breathe.

An object was swinging toward him. A cudgel of some sort. He tried to sidestep it, but the club came crashing into the side of his head. Then he felt his knees buckle, and he was falling, desperately trying to fight off the blackness that was already engulfing him.

* * *

Even from a distance, Camillus could see that something was not quite right in front of the church. He strained his eyes to make out what the object was. It was moving. An animal perhaps? No, it looked too big for that.

A person then? Yes, he realized, it was a man, struggling to stand. By his faltering movements Camillus could tell that the fellow was either badly hurt or dead drunk. One or the other. Cautiously he moved his hand to the hilt of his dagger, but nonetheless rushed forward to see if he could help.

By the time he had almost reached him, the other had managed to stagger to his feet, but instantly crumpled back down. He was clutching his side, as if in pain. No, this was no drunkard. This man had been injured. And quite seriously, by the looks of it.

Camillus halted in front of him, then froze with shock upon realizing who it was. Dropping to his knees beside his friend, he quickly searched for wounds or blood. But it was too dark to see!

"Was it a knife?" he asked urgently.

"No", Curzio somehow gasped.

That violent, uncontrollable shaking. It wasn't a good sign. Not good at all. Fear seized Camillus. Concussion? Had he been struck in the head?

"Where did they hurt you?" he demanded. "I have to know!"

His breathing. That wasn't right either. Much too uneven, too labored. Camillus realized he was on the verge of losing consciousness.

"Don't black out, Curzio!" he begged. "Try to fight it! Do you understand me? *Fight it!*"

Numbly the other nodded. Yes, he understood.

But he couldn't fight it . . .

It was impossible.

XV.

"Signor de Lellis?"

Camillus hadn't realized anyone else was in the room until he heard the voice. He raised his head. One of the doctors was standing beside the chair.

"Is he coming around at all?"

"No", Camillus answered miserably.

The doctor stepped to the bed and checked the vital signs again. He turned back to Camillus and forced a smile. "Everything will be fine", he said. "Try not to worry so much."

"What do you mean, don't worry! He's been unconscious forever! You're a doctor. Can't you do anything about it?"

"I'm afraid not. We just have to be patient, and let nature take its course. I'm sorry."

Camillus wanted to flare at him. But no, he knew that wouldn't be fair. The doctor was doing all he could. It was just this waiting. Sitting there waiting, so helplessly. Exactly as it had been all those months ago, watching his father die.

His father. The sudden comparison startled Camillus. Never had two men been more different than Giovanni de Lellis and Curzio Lodi! Had he actually compared his worry for this innocent and devout friend to that for his beloved father? Incredible! Yet it was true. Camillus had never realized before just how deep a friendship had grown between them. And what if Curzio didn't pull through? What if Camillus lost him as well? The thought was awful, and he forced himself to push it away.

The doctor was looking at him with concern. "I really

think I'd better send in another attendant to replace you. Go to bed yourself."

"No", Camillus objected. "I'll stay."

"You've been here all night and half the day. You're exhausted."

"I said, I'll stay."

The other sighed. "Be prudent, Signor de Lellis. I understand how upset you are, but I don't want you to end up a patient yourself."

"I'm already a patient myself, and I'm not leaving!"

The doctor had to hide a smile and wondered fleetingly why his colleagues were so set against this hard-headed young orderly. He patted Camillus on the arm and gave in. "All right. I'll see that your name is taken off tomorrow's roster as well. You can stay. But tell me if you change your mind."

"I won't change—"

"I know, I know! You don't have to say it. You won't change your mind. Somehow I didn't think so." He shook his head, exasperated. "I'll check in again later. Keep trying to reduce that swelling. I have no idea what they hit him with, but one thing is certain: he's going to have a mighty headache for quite some time."

Camillus nodded and once again soaked the cloth in the basin of cold water. As he was applying it to the ghastly bruise, he could hear the doctor leaving. Why, he wondered, was it taking so long for Curzio to regain consciousness? Surely by now he should have! It had been over twelve hours.

"Wake up, Curzio!" he implored, "Just wake up, will you?"

Helpless. That's how he felt. Entirely helpless.

But was he really? No, he knew he wasn't. He hadn't known it at his father's bedside, but he knew it now. On impulse he reached into his tunic with his free hand and took out the little crucifix given him by his uncle, which for some reason he always kept with him.

Yes, praying was one thing he could do to help his friend.

* * *

Curzio's head was pounding violently. He opened his eyes and tried to focus. But everything was whirling around, and it only made him dizzy. Quickly he shut his eyes again. Where was he? He was lying down, he knew that much. But why couldn't he move? Why did he feel such pain everywhere?

"It's all right", his unspoken question was answered. "You're back at the hospital."

He tried to think. Not an easy task. He recognized the voice. "Camillus?" he asked.

"Yes, I'm right here. How do you feel? That is, apart from half-dead?"

"Dizzy."

"Half-dead, and dizzy. Is that all? Well, I guess that's not too bad, considering."

"Considering what?" Curzio moaned, forcing himself to open his eyes again. "What's the matter with me?"

"You're going to be fine", Camillus told him. "Just try not to move too much. You've had a concussion."

"My side hurts."

"Not surprising. Cracked rib cage. Now, listen, I'm going to help you sit up a little and take a drink. Easy now . . . just go slowly."

"I couldn't go quickly if I tried."

The drink seemed to help. At least the room stopped spinning. "I remember now", Curzio said weakly. "I was attacked, wasn't I?"

"Yes."

"But . . . I don't understand. You were there."

"No, I wasn't. That is, not in time anyway. I'm sorry, Curzio. I really am. Those barbarians beat you badly."

"It wasn't your fault."

"What on earth were you doing out there alone anyway? You know that area isn't safe, especially at night."

"I guess it wasn't very wise", Curzio admitted. "I haven't really been thinking straight ever since we—"

He stopped. No, that wasn't the right thing to be saying. Here he was, sticking his foot straight back into his mouth again, reminding Camillus of their awful argument. He grimaced at his own stupidity and hoped Camillus hadn't caught it.

But Camillus had caught it all right. Curzio saw him look away. "Then it *was* my fault, after all! I should've known!" He got up miserably and turned to leave. "I'll go tell the doctor you're awake. You don't want me in here anyhow."

"No, wait! Please."

Reluctantly, Camillus turned back around.

"I shouldn't have said that. It was thoughtless of me." Curzio sighed. "I say a lot of stupid things that I don't mean to. But at least let me thank you. It must've been you who brought me back here, right?"

Camillus gave him a wry smile. "With the help of a few of my cutthroat sailor friends", he answered bitterly. "The more sober ones, that is."

Curzio stared at him. Those ruffians had actually helped?

Camillus misread his surprise. "Look, I know what you're thinking! But I was afraid to move you too far! I couldn't tell where you were hurt. The docks were closer than the hospital, so I figured it'd be safer to take you there instead."

"That's not what I was thinking. Honestly. And it's not true that I don't want you in here." Curzio paused. The effort to speak was becoming too much. He forced himself to continue. "I'd be grateful if you could thank your friends for me the next time you see them. Will you do that? Please?"

"No", Camillus retorted. "Do it yourself."

Curzio was taken aback by what seemed like sudden rudeness. But then he saw Camillus avert his eyes with shame and explain, "There isn't going to be a next time, Curzio. I'm not going to the docks anymore. I promised God to stay away from there, if only He'd let you live."

Curzio tried to think of something to say, but he had no time. His repentant friend quickly turned away and made his escape from the room.

XVI.

"Glad to see you're finally starting to get your appetite back", Camillus commented cheerfully as he collected the empty dishes onto a tray. "Good sign."

"An appetite for hospital food is a good sign?" Curzio asked. "Actually, I think it must be a bad sign. Better send for a doctor. I'm having a relapse."

Camillus grinned. "You don't have relapses with broken bones, you numskull. Besides, I haven't got time to search for a doctor right now. One's already searching for me."

Curzio looked at him quizzically.

"Well, not just me. Most of the orderlies from our quarters." Camillus shrugged. "Doctor Moretti's called some kind of an impromptu meeting in his office. Don't ask me why."

"A meeting? You can't be serious. Moretti doesn't waste his valuable time giving talks to his employees. It must be something important."

"Don't worry about it. I'm sure it doesn't concern you. Your official status at the moment is patient, not staff, remember?"

"Maybe I'd better go anyhow."

"I'll tell you what happened later, I promise. You're still too weak to get up. Stay in bed."

"This bed is becoming more like a prison. Do you have any idea how boring it is to lie here and stare at these same four walls for days on end?"

"Well, that's what happens when you insist on getting your skull cracked."

Curzio made a face at him. "Doctor Moretti's office is just down the hall. I'm sure I can walk that far if you'll give me a hand. Besides, now I'm curious."

"All right", Camillus gave in. "It's up to you. But I know I certainly wouldn't go if I didn't have to! You should've seen the look he gave me the last time I saw him. I'm sure he burned a hole through me somewhere . . . I just haven't found it yet!"

"Uh-oh. Talk about bad signs!"

"Hey! I've been behaving myself lately!"

"Of course you have. You've been too busy looking after me day and night to get into any trouble." Curzio smiled gratefully and added, "Now, I know from experience why you have the reputation of being the best nurse here."

Camillus grinned back. "One of the best *two*, you mean", he corrected. "And if you really thought that, then you wouldn't look so worried. This meeting can't have anything to do with me personally."

Curzio desperately hoped Camillus was right, but in his heart he still feared the worst. No, this was definitely one meeting he didn't think he should miss.

* * *

"So, de Lellis, I see you've managed to drag at least one friend along", Moretti said sarcastically the minute the two came through the door. "Just as well, as I doubt very much that any other man in this room is willing to stick his neck out for you."

Bewildered by the unexpected greeting, Camillus looked at the handful of other orderlies already gathered there. It was obvious the doctor had been speaking to them beforehand. Why were they all glaring at him with such resentment?

"What's going on here?" he asked, confused.

"Believe me, that's a question I've been asking myself for quite some time now", the doctor replied curtly. His gaze traveled around the office, penetrating each of his employees. Guilt was stamped on all their faces. Moretti cleared his throat and continued. "Have you any idea, de Lellis, the amount of precious time I've wasted this afternoon because of you?"

Camillus glanced at Curzio, who looked worried but equally confused. He turned back to the doctor and decided it might be wise not to answer the question.

"Well, I shall tell you anyhow. I've been engaged in treating two of your co-workers for rather nasty wounds sustained in a fight, which took place between themselves. Within the walls of this very hospital, I might add."

"What does that have to do with me?"

"It has everything to do with you! Perhaps you'd care to speculate what prompted this outbreak of violence?"

"Not particularly", Camillus answered with caution.

"I'll even give you a hint. It was a monetary matter."

Camillus held his tongue.

"A disagreement over a gambling debt, to be more precise", Moretti announced, fuming. "This is the first time in the history of San Giacomo we've ever had to deal with such an outrageous problem! It is likewise the first time we've had repeated incidents of employees staggering in late for work reeking of alcohol and so hung over they can't perform their duties properly . . . you yourself being the prime offender. All these things are a scandal—an insult to this institution and every other hospital in Rome! Do you think I'm totally blind, de Lellis? Do you think I don't know you've been corrupting this place? First by smuggling in kegs to my patients, and then enticing my workers to gamble, and drink, and even brawl in the very corridors of my wards!"

Camillus could feel the hostile stares from all the others. He tried to think of a way to defend himself, but knew it would not work. Moretti was right, no one in the room would cover up for him. No one except Curzio. But why should *he* bother, when he'd been warning Camillus of this all along?

But to his astonishment, Curzio did speak, did attempt to cover up for his misdeeds. "You can't make accusations like that without sufficient proof, Doctor", he challenged, a defiance in his voice that Camillus had never heard before. Indeed, Curzio never defied anyone! And certainly not Doctor Moretti, of all people! Camillus looked at him, surprised and immensely grateful. But there was no time to try to thank him now.

"Proof, Signor Lodi?" the doctor echoed. "You demand proof? Oh, I'll give you plenty of that!" He stood up and jerked open one of his drawers. Triumphantly he threw a deck of cards onto the desktop. He reached in again and withdrew first one flagon, then another.

"Recognize these dear little treasures, de Lellis?" he asked. "You should, you know. They were found hidden among your belongings."

Camillus instantly flared. "Listen here! You have no right to go searching through my things!"

"A search wasn't necessary, I assure you. It's amazing how cooperative others can be in revealing secrets when their own positions are at stake."

Camillus glanced at his co-workers with disgust. "You bunch of stinking cowards!" he snarled. "Can't even answer for yourselves!" He looked back at the doctor. "You can't put all the blame on me!"

"No, I most certainly can't. And I don't. It's myself that I blame, de Lellis. I'm the one responsible for employing you here. I should have followed my instincts. The very moment I laid eyes on you, I knew you were nothing but trouble, fresh from the gutter!"

Even Curzio flinched at the cruel insult. Standing so close to Camillus, he could almost feel his friend's anger being unleashed. He quickly reached over and laid a restraining hand on Camillus' arm. To his relief, he felt some of the tension ebb at his touch.

Nonetheless, he knew he had to do something. Or at

least attempt it! Camillus truly had been trying hard lately; Curzio of all people knew he had! Drawing in his breath, he said the only thing he could think of. "Doctor, it's really not fair to publicly humiliate—"

"Stay out of it, Signor Lodi!" Moretti snapped. "Unless, of course, you relish the idea of making your home in the gutter as well! Because, believe me, I'm in no mood to listen to your useless prattling right now! You know as well as I do that he's as guilty as sin!" The doctor returned his gaze to Camillus and pointed to the door. "Get out of this hospital, de Lellis! *Out!*"

Curzio made one last desperate effort. "Please, Doctor Moretti," he pleaded, "you can't just—"

"Oh—yes—I—can! And I'll do it to you as well if you refuse to hold your tongue!"

Camillus looked at his friend, torn between anger at Moretti and gratitude toward Curzio. With an effort he forced his voice to soften. "He's right, Curzio. Stay out of it. Don't put yourself on the line for my sake. You know more than anyone else that I'm just not worth it."

"Camillus! That's not—"

But Camillus had already turned back to the doctor. He was struggling to remain calm. "All right, I'll go. But first give me my gun. It belonged to my father, and I want it back!"

"So that you can help your Muslim friends murder still more innocent Catholics? Not on my conscience, de Lellis!"

That was too much. Just too much. Camillus couldn't restrain himself any longer. In one quick movement, he sprang at the doctor and grabbed him by the throat, shoving him hard up against the wall.

Moretti's eyes widened in instant fear. He had no doubt that Camillus could break his neck at will if he so chose. For once, he looked entirely helpless, and not just a little terrified.

Every other man in the room froze, too petrified themselves of Camillus' size and strength to dare interfere. Even Curzio was at a loss.

Camillus held the doctor there for long, dangerous seconds, battling the rage within him. But, no. He couldn't lower himself to such violence against a defenseless man. It wasn't right, no matter how strong the temptation might be!

He released his brutal grip, and the doctor stumbled to the floor, gasping for air. Camillus knew he had to get out of there—and fast—before he had time to change his mind. He longed to say good-bye to his faithful friend; he owed him so much! But Curzio had witnessed this last act of weakness—of slavery!—and Camillus was suddenly too ashamed to face him again.

So he did the only thing he could. He turned abruptly and left the room—and San Giacomo Hospital—with nowhere else in the world to call home.

3. The Battle 🐋

XVII.

THE MEDITERRANEAN, 1573 / The very earth itself seemed to pulsate beneath the steady, relentless marching of thousands of men-at-arms. Indeed, the hillside was a throbbing, swarming mass of activity as far as the eye could see, while the troops mobilized into position.

From the summit of the hill, the plain below appeared to be a vast, glimmering sea of armor as the high afternoon sun reflected off countless swords and shields. The battle had been raging for hours, and soon the next wave of soldiery would be sent in as reinforcements.

Camillus knew he should be readying himself for the moment the command would come. All around him the atmosphere was charged with an almost tangible energy as the men tensed like ravenous dogs waiting to be unleashed. But his heart wasn't in it this time. If only he weren't hindered by that accursed leg of his! The wound had recently reopened, and try as he might to ignore it, the pain was becoming intolerable. He'd managed to put up with it all this time, as he'd drifted in and out of various armies for the past year and a half. But now he felt he'd reached his limit.

Wearily, hardly caring anymore, Camillus fell out of line and limped over to a large boulder nearby. No one would notice, so occupied were they with their own thoughts and preparations. He just had to take the weight off it, for however brief a moment. Hours of trekking through this rough, wild terrain was enough to make even a strong pair of legs ache; for him it had been a nightmare.

"How do you plan to fight if you can't even stand on that thing?" a voice inquired from behind. So, someone else had noticed after all. A stocky young soldier came and stood a little unsteadily in front of Camillus. His voice was gruff, but the question hadn't been a taunt. It was sincere.

Camillus shrugged. "I'll manage." He hoped it was true. Long experience had taught him that adrenaline could work miracles in the thick of battle.

His comrade squatted down and studied Camillus with narrowing eyes. "Do the powers-that-be know they're doling out good money to a lame soldier?" he asked with candid curiosity.

Camillus raised an eyebrow. "What do you think?"

"Me? I think you'd better come clean before you're herded off this hill into that ugly mess down there. You don't really look up to it, if the truth be known."

"I'll be fine", Camillus said. "Besides, I wouldn't miss my chance to run a few more Turks through with my sword for all the money in the world!"

The other shrugged. "Suit yourself, friend." He reached into his jacket and pulled out a flask. Handing it over he offered, "Here. Try a drop of this." He gave a conspiratorial wink. "My magic potion. One-hundred-percent guaranteed to dull the pain every time."

Camillus took a quick whiff of the contents and grimaced. "I'm sure it does!" he agreed wholeheartedly, handing it back untouched. "No doubt it dulls a lot of other things as well. Thank you, but no. I'm planning to walk away from this scrap alive!"

The soldier frowned and smelled the drink himself with

such concentration that Camillus had a strong suspicion its contents were already quite diminished. After a moment the man replaced the top, put the flask away, and announced with great solemnity, "Sensible decision. Very sensible indeed."

Camillus couldn't resist a grin.

The thundering of hooves could be heard now approaching behind the troops. With a resigned sigh, the soldier rose. "Well, sounds as if it's time to move out."

Camillus nodded and struggled to his feet.

"By the way," the other informed, almost as an afterthought, "the name's Tiberio Federico Alberto Sicca-Igino Griordini." He paused and gave Camillus a tipsy smile. "My friends just call me . . . Ty."

Camillus laughed, unsure whether or not to believe him, and countered, "Camillus de Lellis."

"Well, best of luck, Camillus de Lellis. Looks like you'll need it."

"Probably not as much as you", Camillus answered with amusement.

Ty lifted his hand in a friendly salute and sauntered away to fall in with the ranks. With an effort, Camillus followed suit.

* * *

After the deafening clamor of battle for hours on end, the valley now seemed as hushed as a vast, open cathedral under the darkening sky. Camillus wondered, numbly, if he was the only man left alive in the world. Everywhere, as far as his burning eyes could see, the ground was strewn with blood-drenched corpses heaped upon one another like discarded rag dolls. And yet, he was vaguely aware that he couldn't be the sole survivor. In the distance there were other stragglers, stumbling through the field like himself, as though sleepwalking. But they all seemed so far away. Everything seemed so far away, so unreal. It was like moving through some horrible, appalling dream.

He bent down to pick up a fallen musket and leaned upon it to ease the crushing agony in his leg. He stood there, dazed and battered, wondering if he had any reserves of strength left to go even a single step farther.

Reaching up, he tried to wipe some of the trickling blood from his eyes and realized dully that his sleeve was soaked scarlet as well. Whether it was his own blood or someone else's Camillus neither knew nor cared. All that concerned him now was to try to focus his hazy thoughts and keep a steady grip on reality, lest he succumb to the shock he knew could be triggered by hours of relentless pain and exhaustion.

He forced himself, by sheer willpower, to take another step forward. The musket made an awkward crutch, but he was grateful for its support.

From nearby a low, anguished moan reached his ears.

Someone, somewhere in this abhorrent carnage, was still alive.

Camillus scanned the ground for a movement, a sign of life, however weak, among the twisted bodies around him.

Nothing.

He waited for long seconds, straining his ears. Yes, there it was again. One living soul among so many dead.

But where?

Camillus knew he could keep going and ignore it. After all, what difference would it make, even if he could find the poor fellow? He was barely able to help himself; what could he possibly do to help another?

But no. He couldn't leave a living man to die, alone and unaided, in this frightful devastation.

He bent down and gently rolled over the soldier closest to his feet. Sightless eyes stared grotesquely up at him, and Camillus let the corpse drop again. Reluctantly he reached for another. It was one thing to fight, and even to slaughter a man in the heat of battle, but a different thing altogether to go picking through the bloody remains afterward.

The next man he turned had been decapitated. For one dreadful moment Camillus thought he was going to be sick. He closed his eyes and waited for the waves of nausea to pass.

And then the voice reached him again.

"Someone. . . ?" It was so soft that Camillus wondered if it wasn't just his crazed imagination playing cruel tricks on him. He looked around with growing desperation.

Then he saw it. A slight movement a few feet away.

He stumbled over to where the man lay and knelt down next to him. The man's face was obscured by blood. Camillus knew he should say something—*anything*—to let the soldier know he was there, but his mind was too exhausted and numb to think of any words. With infinite care, he took the man's head in his lap, unsure what else to do. He could only hope that the mere presence of another human being might do something, however little, to ease his last moments.

The other was struggling to speak. "Are . . . you . . ."— he paused, unable to go on, suffocating with the effort. Camillus knew the man was choking on his own blood. He waited, helplessly. At last the man continued, his voice imploring, beseeching, ". . . a . . . priest?"

The unexpected words ripped through Camillus like a

dagger. For a crazy moment he was certain he was looking, not at the face of a stranger, but at that of his dying father, lying in anguish upon his tear-drenched pillow.

Camillus? Son . . . ? A priest . . . Please, my son . . . a priest . . .

The parting words with which his father had left him.

They seared through his mind, through his heart, again and again, like waves crashing upon him, until they threatened to overwhelm him entirely.

No, he realized . . . *he'd been wrong.* So *terribly, dreadfully* wrong! His presence here could do nothing for this soldier—this immortal soul—held so helplessly on his knees. This man was someone's father, someone's son, someone's closest friend. But their presence would no more have helped him had they been here than Camillus' could . . .

The man was dying. Precariously balanced on the brink of eternity. Heaven or Hell, forever and ever . . .

And all that mattered—*all that mattered!*—was that he, Camillus de Lellis, was not a priest!

He swallowed hard. No words in his life had ever been so difficult to get out. "No . . . I'm not."

The soldier let out one more deep, anguished groan, before his head rolled, lifeless, in Camillus' lap.

How long he continued kneeling there, cradling the dead man on his knees, Camillus had no idea. He had no strength left to rise. He hadn't even the will left to try anymore. Every fiber of his being was defeated, utterly exhausted. He knew, somewhere in the cloudy regions of his mind, that he should say a prayer for this man's soul. He wanted to, and yet . . . even the effort of that seemed beyond his strength.

A hand touched him on the shoulder. He tried to look

up, but couldn't raise his head. He sensed two comrades there beside him, yet they were endless miles away. They were saying something to him, their voices soothing and gentle, but his mind could not comprehend the meaning of their words.

He felt them pulling him to his feet. Funny, even the pain now seemed distant, as if it somehow belonged to another. He could feel strong arms supporting him on either side, and submissively leaned upon them, vaguely aware that without them he would collapse. The men were urging him forward; he tried to resist. The effort to move was just too overwhelming . . .

And then he knew nothing but darkness.

XVIII.

He was drowning.

The water filled his mouth, forcing its way cruelly down his throat. He tried to fight it, tried to force it away. It was suffocating him, annihilating him.

But . . . it wasn't water. It couldn't be. Water didn't burn like this. No, it was something else. He was drowning in a sea of something else . . . much worse.

Camillus had no choice. He had to swallow it. It felt like fire. At last, he gagged it down. His breath came in choking gasps. It wasn't as easy as he'd remembered breathing to be. In fact, nothing was quite like he remembered it to be.

"I think he's finally coming around."

There was a voice somewhere. Someone was lifting his head. And then that terrible, flaming *something* was being poured into his mouth again.

With a tremendous effort, Camillus turned his head and angrily spat it out. He forced his eyes to open. There was nothing but searing light floating shapelessly around him. But then, slowly, the light resolved itself into a blurred face. And a flask. So that was the instrument of torture.

"Easy now. Take another drink", the voice was saying.

No. He couldn't! He couldn't possibly bear it again! He lifted his hand and thrust the flask away with as much strength as he could muster. There was a thud and then the sound of shattering stoneware.

"Are you trying . . . to . . . kill me?" he somehow blurted out fiercely.

His only answer was a laugh and an amused comment, "You're right. He's definitely coming around."

The voice was familiar. A vague feeling of relief washed over him. He realized it was his old friend Antoni.

A second man spoke, slightly less familiar, and definitely less amused. "Do you think he has any conception whatsoever of how expensive that stuff was!"

Camillus followed the sound with his eyes. Another misty face took shape. He could see now he was in a tent, the other two looking down at him.

"I doubt he's terribly concerned about that at the moment, Ty. Send him the tab later." Then, turning back to Camillus, Antoni asked, "How're you feeling?"

Stupid question. How did they think he felt?

"Take . . . three guesses!"

The two soldiers glanced at each other and grinned. "He can't be feeling all that bad. That's my first guess", Tiberio replied.

Antoni said, "Lie down again, Camillus. You've lost a lot of blood. Save your strength for when you need it."

"Which unfortunately", Ty added, "won't be long from now."

Camillus tried to speak. Every word took an effort. "You two are doing one admirable job of cheering me up."

Tiberio shrugged. "That's our specialty."

"Just for once in your life, Camillus—I know it's never come easy for you!—but do what you're told, and lie down again."

Obediently Camillus let himself sink back down onto the blankets on the ground and tried to figure out what he was doing here, why everything hurt so much.

Of course. The battle. He'd been in a battle.

"Did . . . we win?" he asked, confused.

"For the time being we did. Certainly sent a lot of Turks to meet their Maker", Antoni answered.

"But not enough of them yet", Ty said. "Army's on the move again tomorrow at sunrise. That gives you just under eighteen hours to make a sensational, earth-shattering recovery. Think you'll pull it off?"

Camillus groaned. "The good news just never ends. I suppose I don't have many options, do I?"

"Think we'll just abandon you to your own devices? Because if you do, then you insult me!" Antoni tried hard to look offended, but couldn't quite manage. "You and I have known each other since we were seventeen. In all those long years, Camillus, have I ever once let you down?"

"Yes. Countless times." Camillus smiled weakly. "As my partner in a card game."

Antoni lifted his hands in humble surrender. "Apart from those minor catastrophes?" he urged.

"No."

"I'm glad you see it my way. Oh, and in case you're wondering—which I wouldn't blame you if you weren't, this obnoxious fellow here is Tiberio Alberto Signicci Something-or-other."

"I know. We've met."

"Well, then, social formalities over, I'd highly suggest you get some sleep. But this time, Camillus, do me a favor. Try to stay conscious while you do it. You've had us pretty worried since last night, you know."

"My profound apologies", Camillus said, making a face at him. "I'll try to be more considerate the next time I'm nearly killed."

"Apologies accepted."

"One more thing, Antoni. The last time I saw you, back at Signor Vitali's inn a few years ago, you were on your way to Venice to enlist with that buzzard-faced friend of yours, whatever his name was."

Antoni stifled a laugh. "You must mean Dario Tellini. And I admit he didn't think very highly of you and your father at the time either. Not when you told us what side you'd been fighting on for a couple months there."

Camillus felt that old familiar guilt gnaw at him. He avoided the subject. "Anyhow," he asked, "how did you end up here?"

Antoni grimaced with disgust. "You never heard? The dirty Venetian swine went and signed a peace treaty with the Turks. Our company was disbanded." He shrugged. "So most of us decided to hire ourselves out to the Spaniards. And, well, here we are, in the service of His Majesty King Philip the Second. By the way, is your father with us somewhere?"

"No", Camillus answered reluctantly. "He didn't make it."

"Oh. I'm sorry. He was a good soldier."

But Camillus was no longer listening. He could feel the blackness suddenly taking over again, mercifully enveloping him in its dark folds, where there was no more pain.

XIX.

"Have I got news for you, Camillus!" Tiberio announced with great satisfaction as he swaggered over to the small band of mercenaries sitting near the fire.

Camillus didn't bother glancing up. He was studying the cards in his hand intently and didn't want to lose his concentration. "Good news or bad news?" he asked absently.

"Ah! Well, y'see . . . that all depends rather heavily upon one's viewpoint", Tiberio began with his usual drunken solemnity. "Now, from the viewpoint of those dastardly Turks out there, I'd definitely have to say it was bad news! On the other hand, from the viewpoint of those Spaniards, well . . ." he screwed up his eyes in reflection, "at a guess, it's probably good news."

The soldiers at the table exchanged glances of amusement. Camillus indulgently lowered his cards and looked at his friend. "To be honest, Ty, I'm really just thinking about my own viewpoint."

"Ah! From your viewpoint, Camillus . . ." he paused, analyzing it all in his own rather fuzzy mind. "Well . . . I guess it might be good news, or, then again, it might be bad news. All depending. It's really just a matter of your viewpoint."

"Sorry, Camillus, it's no pay raise, that's for certain", Antoni cut in.

The men all laughed.

"All right, Ty. Forget about viewpoints. Just hit me with it."

Tiberio lifted his flask in the air for emphasis, reveling in the fact that he held everyone in such suspense. "Rumor has it, Camillus de Lellis," he began importantly, "rumor has it that tomorrow morning, when we go out there to mince up a few more beloved Infidels, you're being shunted up to the front line."

The grin on Camillus' face instantly vanished. "That's impossible, Ty. Everyone knows they don't put mercenaries on the front line." He glanced around at the others uncertainly. "We can't be trusted, remember?"

"Well, Camillus, they're obviously ready to toss caution to the wind in your case", Tiberio answered with a shrug.

"Looks as if last time you fought a bit too well for your own good", Antoni volunteered. "See, the trick is to fight well enough to keep them happy, but not well enough to be noticed. Takes some skill!"

"Trick is to stay alive, if you ask me!" Camillus returned with feeling.

"Then you obviously stayed alive a bit too noticeably", Antoni reasoned.

"Haven't you figured it out yet, Camillus?" Tiberio explained. "The way our commanders reward a good soldier is by giving him a few more nice, hard hours of fighting, for his utmost pleasure and enjoyment."

"Aw! I would've preferred a pay raise!"

Antoni indicated the large pile of money that Camillus had assiduously gathered from his friends during the last few hours and smiled ingratiatingly. "Leaving it all to me in your will, are you, Camillus?" he asked.

But Camillus only tossed him a cocky grin. "I don't need a will."

*　*　*

They were everywhere. Surrounding him on all sides, their crescent-shaped swords whipping through the air all around him. The blood was like a red rain upon a surging sea of metal. His arm ached. In fact, everything ached. He wondered how long he'd been fighting. Wondered, too, how much longer he could hold them off. If, indeed, he could hold them off at all.

It is a great grace, Camillus, to realize that death may overtake you, too, at any moment . . . His uncle. His uncle had once told him that.

Why did the words so suddenly force themselves into his memory now, at this crucial moment?

You must always be ready. . .

He fiercely swept his own crimson-stained sword through the man directly in front of him with all his strength. He felt a grotesque jolt and stumbled back with the impact. The man vanished from sight.

You're not a soldier! You're not even a servant! You're nothing but a slave, Camillus!

No! Not now! He had no time for these thoughts now! Another Turk was upon him. The sweat was stinging his eyes, blurring his vision. He lashed out blindly, desperately.

The din itself was deafening . . . the clash of steel against steel, the shrieks and cries as men fell by the hundreds, the clamor of horses' hooves closing in on him. . . . He must block it all out! Block out the terrifying rumble of cannon fire, the sound of bullets rending the air so frighteningly close overhead. . . .

If only he could see! He was fighting by instinct alone,

the incredible instinct for survival that so often seemed to take over in combat. He took a chance and raised his arm to wipe his eyes.

Then what felt like a wall of steel collided suddenly with his own sword. It took all his strength to hold it away, to hold the Muslim's blade away.

The noise alone was excruciating. It was impossible to concentrate . . . yet concentrate he must. He had to focus his mind on his sword! He had to overcome, to conquer!

Then start by conquering yourself!

The crazy thoughts just wouldn't go away! They were crowding in on him, crushing him on all sides, as ruthlessly as these slimy Turks!

Sickening pain suddenly seared through him, and he felt the warm rush of his own blood upon him. He had no time to care. . . . It didn't matter! . . . Keep fighting!

You think you know so much about courage, Camillus?

Shut up, Curzio! Don't you dare preach about courage now! You're not standing here with a maelstrom of steel pelting down! Your body's not being hacked at! You don't have to deal with the revolting reality of warfare! Who do you think you are, Curzio? What could you know!

Well, the truth is, courage comes in a lot of different forms. . . .

Go away, blast it! Go away! Camillus thought savagely. *This conversation belonged to a different lifetime! It has no place here!*

Another mighty slash with his blade, another man crumpling at his feet. . . .

Blood was everywhere. It streamed down his face and his sword. He could taste it in his mouth, feel it on his clothes. It was nauseating. . . . He felt helplessly sick. . . . But no! He had to fight on! Nothing else mattered!

It's not even a battle you have to fight alone. God will help you. . . .

Someone was suddenly at his side. He sensed, rather than saw, that it was one of his own. Then more came, appearing out of nowhere, trying to help him.

Relief swept over him. So, some mighty Spanish commander sitting comfortably in his tent had finally decided to send in reinforcements! How very considerate of him!

That meant he'd been fighting for a long time already.

And the battle was still far from over.

They were all there with him now. Antoni. Ty. Even Dario Tellini. Others too, fighting at his side.

Some were falling. Were they friends? Maybe. There was no time to look now . . . no time to spare them a thought.

You must always be ready. . . . You must always be ready. . . .

Death may overtake you, too, at any moment. . . .

Please, my son . . . a priest . . .

The words came, over and over again. They were battering against his soul.

You must always be ready!

He tried to fight them away, but they would not yield to his will as easily as the Muslims did to his sword.

Was he ready? *Was he?*

Camillus de Lellis knew the frightening answer.

The battle raged on.

XX.

A few smoldering embers were all that remained of the once brightly crackling fire. The night air around them was turning bitterly cold, but the soldiers didn't notice.

They were comfortable with the warmth of alcohol inside them and oblivious to everything save the cards in their hands.

Camillus tilted his head back and drained the contents of his tankard. He automatically pushed it toward Antoni, who was closest to the flagon, but his friend hesitated before refilling it for him. Camillus had been drinking heavily tonight. Even more than usual. Oh, well, Antoni decided at last, it didn't really matter. He poured more in and passed it back.

Camillus took another swig, then, tossing his friend a disarming grin, he triumphantly laid his cards faceup on the table for all to see.

The other soldiers groaned with dismay and threw in their own cards, defeated.

Dario Tellini, alone, angrily slammed his fist down on the table and glared at Camillus.

"All right, de Lellis! What's your game?" he demanded.

Camillus glanced at him, but chose to ignore the accusation. Calmly he swept the pile of money from the center of the table toward himself and took yet another long drink.

Tellini, however, wasn't about to let the matter drop so easily. "You've won every hand we've played tonight", he snarled. "Are the extras up your sleeve, or down your boot?"

Camillus looked up this time, his face darkening with indignation.

The atmosphere instantly turned icy. Threatening. The two locked eyes.

The other men exchanged worried glances among themselves. Ty, as usual, was too drunk to notice much of anything. But everyone else knew that Camillus had put away a few too many. And Dario as well. Not a good combination, these two soldiers. Never had been. They should've known better than to invite Dario to join them when Camillus was in the game.

Camillus' voice was low and calm, and dangerously quiet. "Take that back, Tellini."

Antoni held his breath, and his face broke into a troubled frown. Even Ty seemed to realize belatedly that the game had come to a standstill and people were no longer looking friendly.

Everyone at the table waited helplessly. It was up to Tellini now. *Come on . . . don't be a fool,* half a dozen soldiers pleaded silently. Dario wasn't that bad a fellow. Why he and Camillus had never gotten on, they couldn't figure out. But nonetheless there it was. Something personal, no doubt.

Back down, Dario. He wasn't cheating. . . .

To their astonishment, Camillus even gave him another chance. "I said, *take that back!*"

The seconds ticked by. Rather in slow motion. At last, a drunken smirk came over Tellini's face, and he laughed with derision. "Take it back? Take it back from the crippled son of a traitorous pig father?"

Camillus was already rising, unable to believe his ears. "*What!*"

"You heard me!"

His words were hardly out before the entire table was upturned into Tellini's lap. Cards and money flew everywhere.

Stunned, Tellini tried to clamber out from underneath the mess, but he wasn't quick enough. Camillus was already on top of him.

In a flash, all the others, except Ty alone, who was too drunk, threw themselves into action.

"Whoa, now!"

"Calm down, Camillus!"

It was Antoni and two others, pulling him off Tellini, hauling him away. He fought viciously to free himself from their grip, but the three soldiers overpowered him.

"Get control of yourself, Camillus!"

Antoni's stern command finally got through to him, and Camillus grudgingly gave up the struggle. At last he let out his breath and irritably tried to free his arms. His friends relaxed their brutal hold on him slightly, but refused to let go altogether.

With a bit of assistance from the others, Tellini had managed to stagger to his feet. His expression was dazed, his face already rapidly swelling. But he willingly met his opponent's blazing eyes.

Camillus' breath was still coming in gasps, yet his voice was frighteningly calm, and very deliberate, as he challenged, "Say that from the end of your sword, Tellini!"

XXI.

"Are you sure you want to go through with this, Camillus? In cold blood?"

"I can't back out of it now."

Antoni shook his head in disagreement. "Of course you can. Dario hasn't shown up yet. Probably won't either. Chances are he's too hung over to even remember a single word you said last night." He gave Camillus a warning look and added pointedly, "Nor a single word he said, for that matter."

"Well, he still said it", Camillus answered sullenly.

"Don't be so stubborn, Camillus! I refuse to believe he's the first fellow ever to accuse you of cheating! I mean, your exceptional facility at winning does tend to leave one wondering sometimes. I confess the thought has entered my own mind at various times in the past."

"This has nothing to do with cheating or not cheating."

Antoni looked at him blankly. "You mean to say you *were* cheating last night?"

There came Camillus' cocky grin that Antoni had grown so used to after all this time. "Probably not", he assured him mischievously.

Antoni rolled his eyes with despair. "All right. Never mind", he conceded. "If this doesn't have to do with cheating or not cheating, then what is it about? I fear I've missed something important somewhere along the line. Enlighten me."

Camillus looked at him evenly, and his eyes hardened like steel. "He—insulted—my—father!"

There was a silence as Antoni registered this. "Oh", Antoni said flatly, finally comprehending. After a moment, however, his common sense took over again, and he reasoned, "Look, Camillus, I admit it was a low-class thing for him to say and all that, but be reasonable, you were both drunk. Dario's not that bad! And besides, it's not as if your father even cares anymore what people say about him."

"He might not. . . . But I do!"

Antoni threw his hands up in exasperation and tried one last approach. "Listen, Dario's pretty handy with a sword, you know. I'm warning you, Camillus, this might not be as easy as you—"

But the look in his friend's eyes made Antoni clamp his

mouth shut in defeat. He glanced through the trees and sighed. "Well, too late now, anyhow", he announced. "Here they come."

A small group of soldiers was approaching the clearing. Ty, alone, staggered ahead of the others and joined Camillus and Antoni. The rest of the men halted a few yards away. No one spoke.

Ty took Camillus' arm and pulled him aside. "Here", he suggested, thrusting his almost empty flask into Camillus' hand. "Try some of this. Help steady those frayed nerves."

"There's nothing the matter with my nerves, you fool! Would you put your stupid liquor away, just for once?"

Tiberio looked offended as he sulkily snatched the flask back. Camillus wondered, with annoyance, if he'd ever experienced a sober moment in his life. He pushed his way past him and rejoined Antoni.

Tellini was waiting, his mouth twisted into a conceited smirk. Obviously nothing the matter with his nerves, either. He steadily took a few steps forward.

So did Camillus.

The two duelists faced each other in silence and unsheathed their swords.

* * *

So, Antoni had been right after all, Camillus reflected with growing dismay. Tellini was a much better swordsman than he'd given him credit for. The two gleaming blades collided again. Parry. . . side-step. . . parry again! The powerful swords locked against each other with tremendous force and held for long moments. . . .

Disengage . . . and lateral parry. . .

Tellini was toying with him. Camillus knew it. He could feel it in the way he moved his sword, could see it in the amused glint in his eyes. Another resounding clash of steel against steel. The clamor rang in his ears like thunder. And again. And yet another!

Maybe he shouldn't be doing this after all. Riposte . . . and parry again . . . Camillus' muscles were starting to ache. They'd been at it for some time now, and he knew with a sinking feeling that Tellini wasn't fighting in earnest yet.

Never mind, he assured himself, *I'm not that bad at this either!*

The blades twisted together, locked with awesome power, then twisted back apart. It was becoming more difficult for Camillus to catch his breath, but he could see with satisfaction that, if nothing else, Tellini was at least experiencing a similar disadvantage.

Watch the sword. . . . Keep your eye on the sword.

Tellini was too quick! Camillus winced as the blade suddenly ripped through his shoulder. *Ignore it!* he ordered himself. *Take one glance at it, and you're dead! Watch his eyes, not his sword! Watch his eyes!*

Side-step. Parry again, and lunge! Tellini was the one who now flinched and lost his balance. A dark jagged line appeared across his jaw, but he quickly recovered his footing. Savagely, wildly, he lashed out, and Camillus could only dodge ungracefully, barely avoiding decapitation.

Well, he certainly wasn't toying anymore, Camillus realized with apprehension. Or was it with downright fear?

Tellini was coming at him, sweeping his blade fiercely through the air, back and forth. Parry! Hold it off! Retreat! Retreat another step! Tellini was still coming. . . . The two swords clanged against each other, again . . . and again. . . .

Why on earth am I doing this, anyway? Camillus demanded of himself angrily. *Watch the eyes, not the sword! Why am I doing this?*

Take it back? . . . The crippled son of a traitorous pig father . . . !

But Tellini had been drunk! How many stupid things had he himself said in times of drunken anger?

The crippled son of a traitorous pig father! But would his father be proud of him for doing this? His father, who had broken down with such heartrending contrition on his deathbed . . . what would he think of his boy now?

Thrust! Engage! Hold it steady. . . . Hold it!

Disengage!

Retreat another step. No, not just one! Keep retreating—and fast!

It was true, Camillus thought shakily, he had no right to be doing this in cold blood. This was no battle. This was outright murder! Whoever won would be committing actual *murder*!

The mighty swords were crashing against each other with vicious power and frightful speed. Yes, Tellini was definitely in earnest now, the blood gushing from his face and flowing down his collar. Attack—parry—retreat! Parry again—*no!* It was a feint! Another agonizing jolt shot through Camillus. *Ignore it!*

It was as if the two weapons were endowed with lives and wills of their own, slashing through the air, colliding into each other with incredible impact, pulling apart again. Clattering back and forth, back and forth, their cadence like some morbid sinister dance of death.

It was all his fault, Camillus reproached himself. He was the one who'd asked for this!

Another clash . . . the swords drew apart with staggering force and whipped through the air again. . . .

It was a mortal sin!

Yet another mortal sin! And so many already to account for!

And at one time he'd even promised God to be a Franciscan. He, Camillus de Lellis, had sought to become a humble friar in a monastery!

But . . . that was so long ago! So much has changed! It was all beyond my control, Camillus told himself fiercely.

His life was whirling out of his control! Curzio was right. It was a battle! It was exactly as though his soul was caught in the surge of some ferocious battle!

Lateral parry . . . hold it steady . . . *steady!* And thrust with all his strength!

The heavy sword suddenly flying out of his opponent's hand and spinning through the air. Tellini was propelled backward by the impact and stumbled helplessly to the ground.

In a flash, Camillus was at his throat.

Tellini's eyes widened with sudden terror. The naked steel pressed hard against his flesh. He clenched his teeth and closed his eyes, waiting for the lifeblood to be ripped from him.

Camillus wavered. One twist of the wrist. That's all it would take to slit Tellini's throat open.

One tiny, little movement of his hand.

Camillus was startled to realize that he himself was shaking; his heart was racing with fear. Should he do it? He dreaded his own answer. Could he really do it?

You have it in you to rise above yourself, Camillus. I know you do!

Loyal Curzio. Why couldn't he be here now? Camillus needed him! Needed him desperately!

God will help you! He wants to help you! But He can't unless you let Him!

Tellini was waiting, the blood pouring down his cheek, his face contorted with expectant horror. Waiting . . . just waiting . . . for Camillus' blade to plunge his soul into Hell.

Hell.

Forever. *Eternity!* The fire that would never be quenched!!

Camillus? Son . . . ? A priest . . .

No! *No!* Camillus let out an anguished cry and instantly relaxed his iron grip on the hilt.

A dizzying wave of relief and elation swept over him. This battle had been won! He had conquered himself!

Suddenly a deafening report exploded in his ears like a thunderbolt. Camillus spun around in startled confusion.

The smoke was still floating up from the barrel of their commanding officer's matchlock pistol, as he sat there on his steed with ice in his eyes. All the other soldiers were already standing rigidly at attention. All except Ty, who was making a pathetic effort to hold himself erect.

The duelists had no choice. Camillus obediently rose to his feet, and Tellini scrambled up beside him. They stood together, side by side, at attention, struggling to steady their rasping breath.

The officer dismounted, and his glare pierced first one offender, then the other. There was a tense silence as he studied the two with anger and disdain.

It took an effort for Camillus to stand still and not reach up to stem the flow of blood from his shoulder. His shirt was already dark with the spreading stain. Tellini, too, was confronted with the same problem, but the officer didn't care about their self-inflicted miseries.

At length, he demanded, "Which one of you is responsible for this?"

Camillus hesitated. But no, once again he had no choice. Drawing in his breath, he stepped forward and saluted. "Sir. My father's honor was at stake."

The Spaniard raised a haughty eyebrow. "I see."

He clasped his gloved hands behind his back and began to pace in a slow, deliberate circle around the two offenders. Camillus forced himself to stare straight ahead. He would neither back down nor try to justify himself.

The officer cleared his throat and crisply addressed those surrounding them. "A man may be brave in the field, courageous in the front line. And yet . . . yet inflict more harm upon his own comrades than he does upon the enemy. He is like a poison, flowing through the veins of an army, sowing discord at every turn." He ceased his pacing and stopped directly in front of Camillus, his sharp eyes boring into him. "You, de Lellis, are one such man. The insubordination, constant brawling, lack of discipline . . . Need I go on? And now this," he swept his arm around the scene of the duel, "the deliberate attempt to take the life of a fellow soldier! The regulations are very clear, and you have cause to thank God that your intentions were not accomplished, or your own life would have been forfeit!"

Camillus did not move. He stubbornly kept his head held high.

Tellini indulged in a satisfied smirk, but all the others remained at attention, expressionless. Ty lost his balance, and Antoni swiftly reached over to steady him.

The officer missed nothing.

He glared at Tellini first. "You", he ordered sharply, "report back to camp and get your ugly face cleaned up." Then, turning to Camillus, "As for you, de Lellis," his voice heavy with disgust, "you are henceforth dismissed from this army, and may deem yourself lucky to receive such a lenient punishment!"

Too proud to show any emotion, Camillus briskly saluted to his commanding officer and sheathed his blood-stained sword.

"And you can take your inebriated comrad with you as well! I have no doubt His Majesty the King has wearied of wasting valuable Spanish gold to finance an Italian drinking problem." His eyes pierced Tiberio, who didn't seem to understand. After an awkward few seconds, Antoni gave him a discreet shove on the back, and Ty stumbled forward next to Camillus.

Camillus grabbed his drunken friend by the arm with unusual roughness and steered him away from the band of soldiers and through the trees beyond.

4. The Surrender ᔇ

XXII

ITALY, 1574 / It was a great deal of money. Just sitting there in the middle of the table in this backstreet inn, patiently awaiting new ownership.

Camillus absently ran a hand through his hair and tried hard to decide. He desperately wished he had a drink. All the others did. As a matter of fact, there were a lot of things he wished he had now; that pile of money being not the least of them.

He raised his eyes again and studied his opponents. They were all middle-aged. All civilians. And all had nasty smirks on their faces.

All right, he decided. Take the chance.

"You're bluffing", he said to the one on his right.

The man smiled. It wasn't a particularly endearing smile. "Just try me, soldier boy."

Camillus stared hard at his face. But no, it was impossible to read. He glanced again at his own cards and gained a degree of confidence. "Consider yourself tried", he accepted.

He reached into his leather pouch and his fingers touched a few coins. Very few.

Wonderful. Now what?

He could feel his cheeks burning with shame. Well, no way out of it now. Reluctantly he tossed the measly amount onto the table.

The three others all chuckled derisively.

"Raising it a bit steep, are we?" one of them scoffed.

Camillus glared at them. He could feel himself starting to stew. And quickly at that. Keeping his eyes fixed upon them, he removed the powderflask from his belt and laid it on the table.

The motion of the game progressed quickly as the next man threw still more money onto the pile, followed by the other two.

It was Camillus' turn again.

The game came to a pause as they watched him with amusement in their eyes.

Was the man bluffing? If only Camillus could tell. Usually he could tell!

Finally, slowly, he unsheathed his sword and placed it on the table next to his powderflask.

"You're very sure of yourself, boy", the man provoked.

Camillus gritted his teeth and cast another yearning glance at the money. He needed it. He needed it so badly! And the cards he was holding were good. Not perfect, no, but still very good. He pulled off his jacket, roughly folded it up, and staked it along with the rest.

His father had told him never to stake everything he had. He'd usually followed that wise counsel, but this time it was different. He needed to stay in the game! It was his and Tiberio's only chance!

"Got anything else?"

The taunt was almost more than he could bear. He didn't have to take this ridicule! They were playing with a loaded deck, and he knew it!

But, for once in his life, he couldn't figure out how! Oh, what he'd give to have his mastermind father here.

Frantically he rummaged through his pouch. There had to be *something* left! He knew he was looking like a complete amateur. The others could doubtless read his face like a book. If only he could afford even one measly drink to steady him!

His hand closed around an object. He pulled it out, carefully concealing it under the table in order to see first just what it was.

The crucifix.

The crucifix given him by his uncle. He looked at it and swallowed hard. Should he?

For a long, dreadful moment he wavered.

Then at last he slowly put it away and raised his eyes. The decision imparted a certain strange peace. "No", he answered the man quietly. "I have nothing left to gamble."

They seemed satisfied to let him stay in the game. In fact, Camillus could see they delighted in it.

Instantly the action passed to the two gamblers at his left. They bet high.

It was again the turn of the shark on his right. The man reveled in the suspense in which he knew he held Camillus. He took his time about it, looking first at his cards, then next at each of his opponents in turn, pretending to make some momentous decision.

He calmly reached for his goblet and poured himself another drink. He took a leisurely sip.

Camillus could feel his nerves tensing, almost to the breaking point. He hoped wildly that the strain wasn't showing on his face. But he knew that it must be.

The man studied his cards. Took another slow sip of his drink.

Camillus had had enough! "Hurry up, you old fool!" he exploded.

The man wasn't in the least perturbed. He meticulously

flicked a piece of lint off his sleeve and raised that stupid goblet to his lips yet again. When he lowered it, however, he could contain his victory no longer.

"Fool, eh?" he asked, tossing his cards faceup on the table.

The other two bellowed with mirth as they threw in their own cards.

"You didn't do too bad, boy!" the winner managed to choke out amid his laughter. "At least you've still got your shirt!"

If only they knew, Camillus thought to himself, if only they knew how heroic an effort he was making to leave their three scrawny little skulls intact.

He abruptly pushed back his chair and stood up, not allowing himself to indulge in the overpowering temptation.

"Gentlemen", he bid them icily and made his departure from the inn.

The door slammed hard behind him, and he had to lean against it for long moments to calm himself. Those three thieves had no idea how lucky they were that they were still alive!

Tiberio rose quickly from the steps where he'd been waiting and joined Camillus. "And the verdict?" he asked, a hopeful grin on his face.

His only answer was a dangerous look.

"You . . . uh . . . won, didn't you?" Ty ventured, his grin diminishing a fraction. "Please tell me you won, Camillus."

"I—*lost!*"

"But . . . you never lose!"

"Well, I did *this time*, Tiberio!" Camillus announced fiercely. "I lost it all. Everything! You hear me? I said *everything!*"

For once Ty wisely decided to clamp his mouth firmly shut.

Camillus stalked off with a muttered, "Are you coming or not, numskull?"

XXIII.

It was excruciating. Every single step was excruciating! Camillus glared at Ty's back several yards ahead of him and felt his resentment escalating. Why wouldn't Ty slacken his pace? Camillus knew he couldn't possibly keep up with him for much longer! Not with this leg, and certainly not with the steady drizzle of rain turning the ruts in the road into slippery pools of mud.

His eyes traveled to the musket slung so casually over Ty's shoulder, and envy gnawed at him. Should he ask Ty to borrow it? It would at least be something to lean on! He considered it for a long moment, yearning to ask.

But no. He wouldn't admit it to Tiberio. Wouldn't admit that he couldn't keep up with him.

Ty halted and turned around to face him. "I'm going to die, Camillus!" he blurted out miserably. "I swear I'm going to expire at your very feet if I can't have a drink within the next, say, thirty-five seconds!"

Camillus had heard this same complaint over and over again. "Stop it, Ty. You're not going to die from lack of alcohol! It's never been known to happen in the history of the world." He shot him a menacing look and warned, "Keep on complaining though, and you might find yourself perishing from some other cause!"

It was absolute, pure torture! Camillus had hardened himself to pain after so many years of soldiering, but even then, every man had a limit. And his was fast approaching.

Tiberio, however, hadn't taken the hint. "You have no idea, Camillus—you have absolutely no conception whatsoever!—what it feels like to need a drink so badly!"

"Oh—yes—I—do!" Camillus assured him with all his heart. "I also know what it feels like to need food in my belly, dry clothes on my back, and a roof over my head! Now, will you just be quiet!"

Ty spun around and started walking again, even more quickly to show his irritation. Camillus' heart sank, but he doggedly kept going.

"You know what we really need?" Ty asked. "What we really need is to locate ourselves another army to join."

Camillus' reserves of patience were nearing exhaustion. "Sure, Ty. It's that easy. Any minute now some army will come marching down this very road, just begging us to hire ourselves out to them. We can even take turns sharing the same sword! Wouldn't that add an interesting twist to the next battle we find ourselves in?"

In the back of his mind, he reflected with regret that it had been in circumstances not dissimilar to these that he and his father had consented to hire themselves out to the Turks. Men could do strange things when they were hungry and desperate enough. He hoped God had forgiven him for it.

He wondered what he'd do if the sultan's army really did come trooping down this road in front of them. Would he offer them his services again? Camillus knew in his heart that the answer was no. And the knowledge afforded him some small consolation.

"I'm so desperately hungry, Camillus!" Ty moaned now.

Once again he stopped walking and unslung his musket. He regarded it with annoyance and muttered, "Useless thing! What's a gun good for if you can't even use it to hunt?"

Camillus stared at it longingly. He could think of at least one good use for it! But not for the world would he ask.

Ty continued. "Did you really have to gamble away all my gunpowder? How could you have been so thick-headed, Camillus? Now I can't even shoot us some dinner!"

Camillus closed his eyes with exasperation. "Before I joined the game, you gave me the gunpowder, remember? I didn't want to stake it. But oh, no! You were so insistent!"

Ty looked at him angrily. "Well, obviously I didn't know you were going to lose!"

Camillus took a deep breath and silently counted to ten. At last he trusted himself to speak. "Fine. Next time you deal with the filthy swindlers, and I'll leisurely soak up the sun on the steps outside!"

"There won't be a next time! We have nothing left to—"

The sky lit up and a deafening rumble of thunder drowned out Ty's words. The two looked at each other with dismay.

"We're wasting time!" Ty announced hotly. "This ugly weather's really going to break. We've got to find shelter."

He shouldered the gun once again and hiked on. Camillus moaned with agony and followed him. The rain suddenly turned into a pelting torrent.

"We're bound to rediscover the lost strands of civilization in a few more miles or so", Ty said over his shoulder. "Come on, quicken your pace, will you?"

Miles! Camillus thought incredulously. Ty was talking about going miles, and he was worried about merely surviving the next step!

Another flash of lightning streaked across the sky, almost directly overhead. Ty turned to Camillus, bristling. "Can't you bestir yourself to move any faster? This isn't a sight-seeing expedition!"

Suddenly Camillus knew he'd reached his limit. He couldn't do it. He just simply couldn't do it anymore. He veered off the road and painfully sank to the ground under a cluster of trees. They offered practically no protection from the downpour, but he was too miserable to care.

Bewildered and angry, Ty followed him, but remained standing. "What's your problem, Camillus!" he demanded. "Are you such an old woman that you have to take a rest every hour?"

For one terrible moment Camillus felt certain he would lose his own control. He clenched his fists and waited for the powerful urge to pass. Tiberio, however, was oblivious to the fact that his own general health was hanging in a delicate balance, and he continued, "Listen, you can have your cosy nap later. Right now we have to keep moving!"

"Hand me your sword, Ty", Camillus ordered, between gritted teeth.

"Whatever for?"

"Just give it to me!"

"Not till you tell me why!"

Camillus could feel the aggravation swelling inside him. "Listen, fool, I'm not going to behead you, if that's what you're worried about! It would be a pleasure, but that's not what I want your sword for."

Ty scanned their sodden surroundings with vexation. "Look! Whatever your project is, it can wait! We need to get out of this weather!"

"*It can't wait!*" Camillus erupted with violence. "*Give me your stinking sword!*"

The two strong soldiers glared at each other dangerously for a long, tense minute.

Finally, with a sinking heart, Camillus realized that he'd have to beg for it. All right, then . . . he'd beg for it!

"Please, Ty", he pleaded miserably. "Just let me borrow it for a minute."

Surprised by the imploring tone in his friend's voice, Ty relented. He unsheathed the blade and passed it over. "Just be quick about it, whatever it is", he requested grudgingly.

Camillus removed his drenched cloak and held it up. With one quick slash he severed a wide strip from it and returned the weapon. Then he cast a resentful glance at Ty and suddenly felt himself burn with overwhelming shame. Why did Ty have to stand there watching him? Camillus didn't want him to see it! He knew it was horribly infected and looked repulsive, even to himself.

He hesitated. If only Tiberio would look away! But no, the longer he waited, the more intently Ty watched him with a mingling of impatience and curiosity.

There was no way around it. Reluctantly, Camillus pulled off his boot and shuddered with the violence of the pain. The wound had never been this bad before.

Instantly Ty's expression changed as he saw the festering ulcer on his friend's leg. He stood there, dumbfounded, as Camillus quickly started to bandage it up with the coarse, wet piece of cloth.

133

"I'm . . . uh . . . sorry, Camillus", he finally mumbled. "I never knew it was that bad." He took a cautious step backward.

"Forget it", Camillus answered with a shrug. He hoped he sounded casual, but he knew his face must be showing his shame. So, Ty had finally seen it. Now Ty knew the appalling truth. Camillus de Lellis was an incurable cripple, and no army in the world would deign to waste their money putting him on their payroll. He forced his voice to remain steady. "Just give me a minute to sit here, all right? We can be on our way again soon, I promise."

Ty drew in a deep breath. "I don't think so, somehow", he said, his words heavy with meaning.

The deep humiliation cut Camillus to the quick. "Then just go on without me!" he blurted out savagely. "You need me to hold your hand every rotten step of the way?" His eyes were like blazing steel, and Tiberio felt a sudden rush of relief that it was he, and not Camillus, who was holding the only sword. He swallowed hard and slowly sat down as well, but made sure to keep his distance.

"Look, I said I was sorry", he repeated. "You know I won't go off and leave you here alone. Like it or not, we're in this mess together."

XXIV.

Well, if nothing else, Camillus reflected bitterly, at least it had finally put an end to Ty's ever-flowing stream of complaints! He had made the heroic effort not to mention alcohol or food even once in all the time they'd sat there, helplessly huddled under their cloaks, waiting for the incessant downpour to pass.

At last, the storm moved on, leaving both men drenched, cold, and feeling not just a little depressed.

Camillus ventured a glance at his companion. As he'd expected, Ty was in a foul temper—and who could blame him? Camillus drew in his breath and managed to mutter, "Well, I guess we can't sit here forever."

Ty nodded, abruptly stood up, and made an angry attempt to wring some of the water from his saturated cloak. Camillus likewise staggered painfully to his feet.

But it was too much. He realized, aghast, that he truly couldn't stand unsupported. The agony instantly triggered off waves of dizziness. Camillus could do nothing but lean against the tree and gingerly lower himself back to the ground.

Mortified by such helplessness, he stole another look at Ty. He could see that Ty was trying hard to be patient, yes. But he could also see that ill-concealed glint of disdain in the other soldier's eyes, and it dawned on him for the first time that Ty was keeping a safe distance away.

Camillus remembered fleetingly that this same man had once helped to save his life. Ty, together with Antoni, had safely brought him back to camp and treated his wounds. But things had been different then. Those had been battle wounds, sustained in honorable combat, not some putrid, diseased ulcer. Camillus hadn't seen Ty's face then, but he knew with absolute certainty that it had not held the hint of contempt it did now.

"You have to get back up again, Camillus", Ty ordered firmly, without, however, making a move to help him.

Camillus swallowed hard. "I can't", he confessed miserably.

"You have to try!"

"I told you, I can't!"

Ty heaved an exaggerated sigh and glanced around. Camillus knew what he was thinking. They needed to find shelter and dry themselves by a fire before night fell. They needed to continue their search for food. Camillus couldn't blame Ty for being annoyed. Who wouldn't be frustrated by the burden of a useless cripple thrust upon him at a time like this?

Yet there were a few men who wouldn't be, Camillus realized with a pang of sadness. His father, for one. With that fiery will of his and that unquenchable spirit, his father would have found a way to brighten up their hopeless situation and take care of his boy.

Curzio was another. Loyal, self-sacrificing Curzio. There would be no scorn or impatience in his eyes! On the contrary, his gentle encouragement would have somehow made even the tormenting pain easier to bear.

Antoni, likewise, would have at least treated him better than this, surely!

Camillus found himself afraid to meet Tiberio's gaze again. What if Ty decided to abandon him after all, to leave him to die of starvation and exposure, out here alone in this rugged countryside? Unable to move, to find wood for a fire . . .

To die . . . alone . . .

His father's tear-drenched face flashed before his mind. His father, begging with his dying breath for his son to fetch a priest.

The lifeless soldier invaded Camillus' memory as well. The one he had held so helplessly on his knees in the bloody aftermath of battle so many months ago. That man too had implored only the presence of a priest.

Suddenly, with frightening clarity, Camillus understood. Understood how they both had felt . . .

A panic that he'd never known before raced through him. He realized with terrifying desperation that he, too, needed a priest. *And badly!*

He raised his imploring eyes to Ty—his only hope—but saw with dismay that Ty was leaving. Actually leaving!

So this was it. Ty was really going to do it. Abandon Camillus to die! *Without a priest!*

Camillus' heart missed a beat. He cried out, "Ty, please!"

Startled by the unexpected anguish in his voice, Ty stopped and turned around. Irritation was stamped all over him.

"Just wait a minute, will you?" he grumbled.

Camillus watched with apprehension as he continued on his way to a nearby tree. What on earth was he doing? Then Camillus noticed that the formation of the tree's trunk had caused a little rivulet of rain water to trickle down. Tiberio was taking out his flask and filling it.

Camillus felt relief surge through him. Ty wasn't leaving after all! That meant Camillus would not die here alone at enmity with Christ and devoid of grace in his soul. He let out his breath and silently thanked God.

Ty returned and squatted down a few cautious feet away, offering Camillus the water. "One-hundred-percent guaranteed not to dull any pain at all," he mumbled in a pathetic attempt at humor, "but you might as well take a swig anyhow."

Camillus gratefully accepted the drink but saw that Ty was still eyeing him warily and made no move to take his flask back. Instead, he moistened his lips nervously with his tongue and rudely asked, "Is that disgusting thing . . . uh . . . contagious?" Camillus knew, of course, that Ty had been thinking it all along, but to hear him voice his revulsion aloud and with such bluntness was mortifying.

Camillus lowered his eyes and managed to mumble, "No."

"You promise?" Ty persisted, unconvinced.

The stab was unbearable. "Yes, I promise!"

Ty considered, then finally said, "All right. But you better not be lying to me!" Stepping closer, he slung Camillus' arm around his shoulders and hoisted him to his feet. "I wouldn't put any weight on that hideous mess if I were you", he advised gruffly. "Just let me take it all."

Camillus could think of nothing to say. He felt Tiberio's strong grip around his waist and, despite the torment of embarrassment, had never been so grateful for another man's strength in all his life.

XXV.

It was obvious that Ty couldn't sleep, either. From where he was lying several yards away, stiff and uncomfortable on the ground, Camillus could sense his companion's rest-lessness.

But neither of the men felt any inclination to talk to the other.

Camillus rolled over, irritated, and pulled his cloak tighter around him. It made a pathetic blanket against the biting night air, but at least it was dry again.

The gnawing emptiness in his stomach was becoming more intolerable with each passing minute. Camillus forced himself not to think about it and determinedly closed his eyes.

But it was no use. He knew sleep would never come. With a sigh of frustration, he sat up and glanced over at his comrade. Ty was lying on his back, morosely staring up at the clear star-studded sky above them. He didn't return the glance.

Camillus picked up the walking stick he'd found earlier and clambered to his feet. The pain was driving him mad, but as with the torment of hunger, he had no choice but to put up with it. Wearily he hobbled over to the dying fire and tossed a handful of dry twigs onto the embers. He poked them with the stick until the kindling broke into flames, then sat down close to what little warmth they would give.

He had no idea where he and Ty were. They'd been making such dreadfully slow progress, traveling at most only a few miles a day. Camillus knew, despite Ty's comments, that it wasn't entirely his own fault; Ty too was weakening now. Day after endless day of surviving on nothing but wild fruit was taking its toll on both of them, and their strength was fast diminishing.

What would become of them, Camillus wondered with despair. He stole another glance at Ty and felt a stab of envy. It wasn't too difficult to imagine what Tiberio's future would hold. Eventually they'd get themselves out of this rut. They'd somehow find food and regain their strength. And then what? Ty could return to his home, his family. He could go back to soldiering; there were dozens of princes and nobles who would accept a strong, able-bodied swordsman like Ty to fight in their ranks. No doubt he'd take to drinking heavily again and suffer the consequences in one form or another until the day he dropped. But what did it matter? At least Ty had a future, Camillus thought, a future within his control.

But what of himself? What future did he have?

He tossed a larger log into the fire and absently stoked it. He had been trying for months now to ignore the future, but he knew he'd have to face it sooner or later.

There was no doubt whatsoever in Camillus' mind that not a single army would ever want him again. Oh, yes, he could still fight with the best of them; he was still an excellent soldier! But one must be able at least to stand in order to fight, and only a completely blind commander would hire Camillus now.

He sighed and lowered his head into his hands. He didn't even have a home to go to. Many years ago, his family had been well-off, possessing land and power. But all that remained now was his noble surname. His father— yes, his beloved father—had managed to lose everything through gambling debts and unprofitable investments.

Where, then, could he go? What could he do?

For a fleeting moment Camillus' mind returned to the Franciscan monastery at Aquila. But he dismissed the thought as suddenly as it had come. No, that wasn't the answer to his miseries. If his uncle had refused him entrance years ago, when his leg hadn't been so bad, then surely he would refuse him now, when Camillus wasn't even able to walk without another man's support. Besides, it was true, the monastery wasn't a place to hide from one's crosses.

On impulse, Camillus reached beneath his cloak and pulled out the crucifix his uncle had given him. He'd never really paid it too much attention all these years. But now he looked intently upon the Figure on the cross by the light of the crackling fire.

Yes, there was One Who understood his poverty, his pain. One Who had also been an outcast, and, likewise, had not even a place to rest His head.

God will help you—He wants to help you! But He can't unless you let Him!

Curzio's words. They came back again, unbidden.

But this time, the words didn't reproach Camillus. Instead, they filled his heart with a glimmer of hope. The first hope he had felt in a long, long time. Indeed, since those very days at San Giacomo, with the help of the only true friend he'd ever had.

Yes, he realized, God was merciful. God hadn't let him die out there in the wilderness a few days ago, without the merits of the Precious Blood to wash his soul.

Camillus knew he must go to confession. He might die of starvation regardless . . . but he'd force himself to stay alive at least until he could find a priest. Somewhere.

He had a reason to keep going now. For once, his stubbornness would serve him in good stead! Of that, he was determined.

At long last, Camillus lay down close to the newly enkindled blaze, and knew that peaceful rest would finally be his.

XXVI.

The carriage rumbled by with such reckless speed that it threatened to run them clear off the road. The two stumbled to the side just in time for the thing to pass. No sooner was it beyond them than they noticed something had been tossed out the window, its contents scattered on the ground.

The two looked at each other, a strange mixture of dread and hope in their eyes. Tiberio waited until the carriage was out of sight before releasing his supporting grip around Camillus, then hastened forward to examine what they both guessed were discarded scraps of food.

Camillus watched as he fell to his knees and began stuffing wads of garbage into his mouth with a frenzy born of desperation. The mere sight of it made Camillus feel sick.

"Come here!" Ty called out, food dribbling down his chin in his eagerness. "There's enough for both of us, but only if you hurry."

Camillus felt his stomach lurch. Loathing every step that brought him closer, he limped over to the heap of trash on the road. He stood there, uncertainly, fighting revulsion. Even the smell was putrid!

Finally he swallowed hard and admitted, "I can't do it, Ty. I'll starve to death before I eat someone else's filthy rejects." But even as he spoke, he knew the words weren't true. He had never been so ravenously hungry in all his life.

Ty looked up and said gravely, "Tell me if you really mean that, Camillus. Because if you do, it just means there's more for me."

An involuntary groan escaped Camillus, but he dropped to his knees on the roadside next to his companion. Gingerly he fingered a few scraps splattered on the ground. Covered with mold and half-consumed, it was impossible even to tell what the stuff was. He stared at it, overwhelmed with repugnance. How could he actually bring himself to eat it?

Yet how could he refuse? How could he deny his starving body whatever little nourishment he could find?

Hating himself for it, Camillus turned his back so that Ty couldn't see and forced himself to eat the first meal he'd had in days.

How, he wondered, had he ever sunk so low?

* * *

The moment the woman saw the two men approaching along the dusty road, she knew she'd ask them. She had to. They were her only hope.

She waited on the grassy verge, protectively clutching her thin, flailing baby tightly against her threadbare dress. The closer the men got, the more her heart raced with fear. She could see now by their clothes that they were soldiers, rugged and unkempt. Their steps were faltering; one was helping the other along. Were they drunk? She couldn't tell from this distance. Only one was armed, but they both looked large and strong, and she so entirely defenseless against them! Still, she had no choice. Whispering a prayer, she bravely stepped forward.

Camillus was the first of the two to spot her. He pulled away from Ty's shoulder and stopped walking. Ty glanced at him, then followed his gaze to the approaching woman.

Before they knew it, she had rushed up to them and cast herself upon her knees at their feet.

"Please," she implored, "have pity on me! My child hasn't eaten for days!" She fearfully lifted her eyes, and the deep sorrow and hopelessness Camillus saw in them instantly tugged at his heart.

For a moment the pair were too taken aback to respond. The young mother continued to kneel there, unable to control her trembling.

Recovering from his surprise, Camillus reached down and pulled her to her feet. "I'm sorry," he apologized softly, "we have nothing to give you."

"Please!" she blurted. "Please, for the love of God!"

Camillus glanced at Ty, unsure what to do. But Ty merely shook his head and stepped around the woman to continue on his way. He halted just beyond her and waited impatiently for Camillus.

Camillus helplessly returned his gaze to the woman. "I'm sorry", he repeated.

The sadness in her eyes was more than he could bear. Yet he knew there was nothing he could do. Despising himself for it, but with no other choice, he moved past her and joined his companion.

Ty stepped closer to offer him assistance, but Camillus irritably pushed him away and hobbled on alone.

"Don't take it to heart", Ty said, annoyed by his friend's sudden touchiness. "There's nothing we could've done for her. We have enough problems of our own."

"Leave me alone."

Ty rolled his eyes. "Really, Camillus. You know as well as I do that it's not our fault."

Oh, yes, it is! Camillus thought angrily to himself. Maybe Tiberio couldn't reproach himself, but he certainly could! He had no one else to blame but himself for the wretched situation he was in. He'd dug his grave, and now he was lying in it. His unconquerable temper. That's what it was! His temper and his pride! He'd wasted every single chance he'd ever had. Thrown out of the hospital, dismissed from one army after another, reduced to utter destitution because he'd been so conceited to think he could always get whatever he wanted.

It was true. He was a slave, he admitted brutally. A slave! That's what he'd been year after year, and now the payoff had come. And what a fitting payoff it was! Starvation for his intemperance in drinking. Poverty for his greed and dishonesty in the gambling dens. Lameness and humiliation for his self-conceit. Yes, he told himself fiercely, he was reaping exactly what he'd sown!

But the most dreadful part of it all was the woman. He'd turned her away, she who had asked for his help. No, not asked. *Begged! Beseeched! On bended knee!* He, Camillus de Lellis, of noble blood, had despicably left a helpless woman alone in her terrible distress!

It was awful. He knew he couldn't live with himself if he didn't somehow aid her.

Turning back, he cried out, "No! Wait!"

The woman stood where they'd left her, her back toward them, dejected. At the sound of his voice, she turned to face Camillus, and he could see her cheeks were damp with tears.

Camillus realized that Ty was staring at him, with something akin to amusement. What did it matter? Ty had already seen him as humbled, ashamed, and helpless as he'd ever be. Let Ty think what he would!

Determined not to limp, Camillus gritted his teeth against the pain and strode back to her. His heart was pounding; he had no idea what he was going to do. Yet he had to do something!

The woman looked up at him, uncertain and afraid. She clutched her baby protectively.

Camillus did the only thing he could. He pulled off the remnants of his cloak, his only expendable possession in the world, and carefully tucked it around the squirming infant.

"I know it's little more than nothing, but it's all I have", he told her. "I'm truly sorry."

"May our Lord reward you, kind sir", the woman replied, gratitude shining in her eyes.

And Camillus felt sure that her words were a genuine prayer.

XXVII.

They knew they had to do it. If they wanted to stay alive, they simply had to do it. It was the most degrading thing either of them would ever do in their lives, and they couldn't even bring themselves to say the word aloud. But they both knew it had to be done.

"You take the church steps, Camillus. It'll spare you from walking. I'll go door to door."

The two exchanged a long, despairing look, each silently imploring the other to think of a way out.

There was no way out. A man could go only so long without food.

Camillus nodded, unable to think of anything to say. Ty didn't expect an answer anyhow. He unslung his musket and handed it to Camillus. "I'll come back when I've got enough for a meal", he muttered miserably.

Again, Camillus only nodded and leaned upon the gun. He watched Ty depart, then limped his way toward the cathedral.

There were other beggars there on the steps as well. Blind. Deformed. Ragged. Some were elderly, others mere children. Most seemed genuine, though doubtless some were fakes. But all looked as desperate as Camillus knew he himself must look.

Painfully he mounted the steps. A few eyed him with suspicion, even open animosity, as if his competition there would be to their own disadvantage. But they soon lost interest in him when they noticed he was entering the church.

If he must beg, then all right, he'd beg. But Camillus knew he had to first beg from Another. Not for money, not for food, but for mercy. For God's forgiveness.

* * *

"I sure hope you did better than I did", Tiberio moaned as he opened his hand to reveal a mere pittance in coins.

To his surprise, Camillus tossed him the first genuine smile he'd seen in months and triumphantly held out a few gold pieces.

Stunned, Ty let out a whistle. "Looks like you struck gold! Literally! How on earth—"

"I'll tell you later. First, let's go and *eat!*"

Tiberio nodded in wholehearted agreement, and the two novice beggars headed straight for the closest tavern. Ty flung open the door, slumped down at a table, and called out to the owner, "Bring us everything you've got! And I mean, everything!"

Astonished, the owner regarded them for a moment, then disappeared into the kitchen, only too eager to cash in on their hunger.

"I don't know about you," Ty said grinning, "but I'm going to sit here and gorge myself all night long!"

Camillus laughed and sat down as well. "And drink too, no doubt?" he countered.

"You better believe it!"

"Well, that makes two of us."

They looked at each other, and Camillus realized that it

was the first time in ages they'd shared a bit of lighthearted banter. Soon the tavern keeper bustled back in, laden with food and drink, and for a few wonderful minutes it was as if all their hardships and animosity of the last few weeks didn't exist anymore. In companionable silence, the two starving soldiers got down to the serious business of eating.

But after wolfing down the first huge helping, Camillus realized that keeping it down wasn't going to be as easy as he'd thought. After being deprived of food so long, it seemed as if his body had forgotten what to do with it. He decided he'd better heed the warning and pushed his plate away. Save the seconds for later.

Ty didn't seem to be presented with the same problem. Camillus watched him with amazement as he stuffed himself with helping after massive helping, greedily reaching for the flagon in between.

Camillus cleared his throat and ventured to warn, "I don't think it's such a good idea to drink so much right now, Ty. Maybe you should wait for a while."

Ty ignored the advice and refilled his goblet to the brim with an eagerness bordering on panic. Camillus merely shook his head.

At length Ty leaned forward and lowered his voice. "You stole it, didn't you?" he asked between chews. "The money, I mean."

Taken aback, Camillus stared at him. "Of course not!"

Ty cast a glance around them. No one was within earshot. "Come now, Camillus. You don't have to play games with me. I know you stole it. You've still got one thing going for you at least—sleight of hand!" He winked and added, "No doubt comes from all those years of practice cheating at cards the way you do."

Camillus bristled. "Look! I didn't steal it, all right? And I don't rely on dishonesty when I win a card game, either! I happen to be possessed of a brain that, unlike yours, actually functions."

Well, so much for the companionable rapport, Camillus thought bitterly.

"You can't fool me", Ty persisted. "No one would give so much money to a beggar."

Camillus sighed. "I didn't beg for it", he explained as patiently as he could. "A gentleman at the cathedral offered me work. I accepted. This money is a couple of days' advance on my wage. Enough to tide me over till I get there."

Surprised, Ty stopped chewing, lowered his drink, and actually had the nerve to laugh. "You must be joking!" he blurted out. "Who on earth would be so stupid as to offer work to a useless crip—" He caught himself and shut his mouth before the word had escaped entirely.

But Camillus guessed it anyhow and felt, once again, the shame he'd endured ever since Ty had seen the wound. He averted his eyes and forced himself to stay calm. "Perhaps the man was blind", he got out between clenched teeth. "I didn't think to ask him."

Ty looked suddenly uncomfortable. "I wasn't going to say . . . I mean, I didn't . . ."

There was a frosty silence. Camillus decided he needed a drink after all and reached for the flagon.

Ty cleared his throat. "Uh, what kind of work?" he pried, curiosity getting the better of him.

Camillus glared at him, unsure whether or not to tell. He had a sinking feeling it would only trigger off more cutting remarks and didn't feel as if he could endure anymore of that just at present.

"Come on . . . what kind of work?"

Camillus sighed and gave in. "There's a Franciscan monastery being constructed in Manfredonia, not far from here. They need laborers."

As he expected, Ty sniggered. "A monastery?" he repeated with amusement. "*You* working at a monastery?" He let out a guffaw. "Hate to say it, Camillus, but it doesn't exactly fit your image!"

"Apparently," Camillus said icily, "I don't have much of an image left these days. You remind me of that every time you open your flapping jaw!"

"Hey! You listen here! I didn't—"

"Quiet, Tiberio!" Camillus warned dangerously. "I may be lame, but, then again, it's not my *leg* I need to bash your ugly face in!"

Ty made a quick decision that it would be wise to back off. He'd seen the results of Camillus' outbursts in the past and had no desire to join the ranks of the victims.

Another uneasy silence ensued. Ty nervously took another drink and tried to gather his courage. "Listen," he muttered, "we're both a bit edgy right now. Let's just calm down, all right?"

"All right."

"You're not . . . uh . . . really going to do this work, are you?"

"Of course I am. I gave the man my word."

"But he already gave you his money!"

Camillus looked at him sharply. "Meaning what?" he asked, although he knew perfectly well the answer.

"Meaning he'll never know if you simply disappear! What's he going to do if you don't show up? Send out a search party of brown robes?"

Camillus felt exasperated. "I gave him my word, Ty", he repeated, with as much patience as he could muster.

Ty had obviously regained his nerve by now. "If you really think a man's word of honor means anything, then you need your head removed and screwed back on the other direction. What's the matter with you, Camillus? Peel the scales off your eyes, and look at all this money! Granted, it's not a fortune, but all we have to do is make our merry way to the next town, get into a game, and with your expertise we'll be rolling in money! You know it's true!"

Yes, Camillus knew it could be. The prospect was definitely attractive.

"Take my word for it," Ty tempted smoothly, "all you need is to find a hospital somewhere. Any decent doctor should be able to fix your leg, and then, presto! You're all set! There are a hundred armies out there who'd fall over backward for a fighter like you! You don't have to become a slave to a horde of monks!"

Slave. Did he have to choose that particular word?

"Listen, Ty," Camillus answered wearily, "all I want right now is a good night's sleep in a real bed. With real blankets and a real pillow. I don't feel like discussing this anymore tonight."

"Have it your way. But you'll see. By the morning you'll have reached your senses." Ty winked and promised, "One-hundred-percent guaranteed!"

* * *

He couldn't believe he was really doing it. Stealing his benefactor's money and leaving town. And not even twenty-four hours after he'd been to confession.

Camillus stopped abruptly and pulled away from

Tiberio's supporting grip. "I can't do it, Ty", he announced with resolution. "It isn't right."

Tiberio lowered the flask in his hand and raised an eyebrow. "Since when has *that* ever governed your decisions?" he asked, his speech slurred.

Camillus chose to ignore the sarcasm. He scanned the ground nearby for a stick he could use for a crutch and wondered with dismay how he'd ever travel back alone. But he knew he must, somehow. He'd done a lot of despicable things in his life, but he'd never been a thief. And he'd never broken his word of honor.

"Good bye, Ty", he said firmly. "Best of luck." He extended his hand.

But Tiberio refused to shake it. He stared at Camillus, incredulous, then slowly a look of scorn spread across his face. He shook his head. "You're a fool, Camillus", he said with amazement. "I'd never have taken you for such an utter fool."

Insult upon insult, but Camillus determinedly held his peace. Tiberio turned and started to stumble drunkenly away.

Camillus knew the food from last night wouldn't last either of them long and, on impulse, called out, "Ty, wait!"

The other turned around, still smirking with amusement. They both regarded each other for a long moment.

At last, Camillus held out the remainder of his money. "You saved my life, Ty", he said quietly. "I owe you. You'll need this more than I will."

Tiberio eyed the coins for a few seconds, then eagerly strode back and snatched them from Camillus' hand. "You're right", he agreed. "You do owe me. I've been your nursemaid for too long already. Let the sweet monks coddle you instead, if you're too much of a coward to fare for yourself like a man."

Camillus flinched at the words. Even the fact that Ty was drunk when he said them didn't cushion the cruelty. But to his own surprise, Camillus realized that the unjust parting did nothing to inflame his pride.

For indeed, Camillus de Lellis had very little pride left anymore.

He stood there and watched silently as Tiberio wheeled around and staggered on, alone, down the road.

XXVIII.

MANFREDONIA, FEBRUARY 2, 1575 / If only the mule would cooperate. He and Camillus had been inseparable companions for close to a year now, yet the obstinate thing still refused to cooperate.

Camillus' patience was wearing thin. It had been a long and taxing journey between the two monasteries with the cartload of building materials, and he was tired. Under the treatment of the kind monks, his leg had improved somewhat, but the exceptionally long walk of this particular day had brought back that old familiar ache, and all he wanted was to return to the cell that was the only place in the world he had to call home. He was in no mood for silly games with a pig-headed beast!

He tugged on the reins with all his might, but the mule only took it as a cue to plant its hooves more firmly on the ground. Camillus sighed. He cast a furtive glance around him, hoping that none of the friars in the distance were noticing this ridiculous struggle.

And that's when he first sensed it.

He could feel it in the earth beneath his feet. That almost imperceptible vibration that he knew oh so well. Yes, it was charging the very atmosphere around him. None of the friars would notice it of course, but he, an ex-soldier, could tell without a doubt.

There was a battalion on the move somewhere nearby.

Camillus scanned the countryside around him, more out of instinct than any real need or desire to see them. But see them he did, a massive shimmering line of armor snaking its way over the horizon.

An unexpected rush of yearning gripped him as he shielded his eyes against the bright sun and watched. Until now, he had never allowed himself to dwell on how much he missed his old life . . . missed the fighting, the adventure, the feel of a heavy sword in his hand and a musket over his shoulder.

He forced himself to tear his gaze away and looked instead at the stupid animal at his side and reminded himself brutally that it was his own fault. No one else was to blame. If only he had stuck it out at San Giacomo all those years ago. If only he had behaved himself and given it time. If only—

But the past was gone. He couldn't change it now. Camillus knew he'd never be a soldier again. A sigh of sadness escaped him, and he dutifully gave the mule's reins yet another pull. The animal, however, simply refused to move.

Suddenly weary, Camillus closed his eyes. He had to push the regrets away; they would do him no good. He had to fight against them.

When he opened his eyes, his heart nearly stopped at what he saw.

Panicking, he searched the ground for a stick. Finding one, he struck it against the mule's hindquarters with ruthless strength.

"Move you useless beast! *Move!*"

It didn't work.

Camillus risked another look over his shoulder. A breakaway group of armed men were coming his way, their steps unsteady, flasks waving drunkenly in their hands. He did a quick calculation; there were about half a dozen of them. No . . . more than that.

Please God, he begged silently, please don't let them recognize me!

But even as he prayed the words, he knew it was too late. Of course they recognized him! Why else would they be approaching in the first place?

He had to get out of here . . . and fast! Frantically, he beat the mule with the stick again. But the creature just rolled a languid eye at him and refused to budge an inch.

"Me oh my, what a surprise! If it isn't Camillus de Lellis himself!" Tiberio called out with drunken solemnity.

He'd done it on purpose. Camillus knew he'd led them here on purpose. He gritted his teeth and waited helplessly as the band of soldiers hopped over the low stone wall and gathered in front of him.

Ty, he could manage. After all, Ty had seen him reduced to much more humiliating and deplorable circumstances than being a mule-driver. Indeed, Ty had even shared some of the degrading shame with him—picking through repulsive scraps on the roadside, begging for money in the streets.

Oh yes, Ty, he could manage!

But the others?

Instinctively Camillus turned his eyes to Antoni for help. His old friend Antoni. After fighting so many battles side by side, after sharing so many memories together through all their years of soldiering, surely Antoni wouldn't berate him in his present lowly position.

But to Camillus' utter dismay, an amused grin spread across Antoni's face, and he said, "That's one very curious sword you're holding there, Camillus. Don't believe I'm familiar with that particular design."

Another man took up the jest and grabbed the stick from Camillus' hand. He held it up and swiped it through the air, and the others all jumped back in mock terror.

"Oooooh! Dangerous, eh?" one of them remarked, as another slowly crumpled to his knees and clutched at his heart like a dying man.

"Whew! Too hazardous for me, this thing", the one holding the stick commented, offering it gingerly to Camillus. "Take it back, please! I'm just not expert enough for a weapon like this!"

Camillus couldn't believe this was happening to him. He felt his heart sink. He didn't dare reach for the stick. The soldier threw it to the ground as if it would bite him, and the others all sniggered.

"Looks like even our heroic Camillus is too afraid to touch it", one of them teased.

Camillus just stood there, feeling the fool.

Antoni came over and put a comradely arm around his shoulders. "Do you really think", he asked, "that you'll, uh, make your way up in the world by taking asses for leisurely strolls through the countryside?"

Camillus couldn't think of anything to say.

"Antoni asked you a question", Ty joined in. "Are you

going to answer him, or have the dear friars unlearned all your good manners?"

Camillus swallowed his pride. "I'm not trying to make my way anywhere", he answered. "A man's got to eat."

"Ooooooh, pardon us!" another said with a wink at his comrades. "He's gone philosophical now, as well!"

"And what's so wrong with army rations, Camillus? Or do you prefer the bread of the poor these days?"

Camillus had had enough. He felt his temper surfacing. His abominable temper, which he'd been trying so hard to conquer all these long months. "Out of my way", he ordered roughly. "I have work to do."

Please, God . . . make the mule move!

His prayer was mercifully answered. The creature finally decided to step forward. But to his consternation the group of soldiers fell into step alongside of him.

"Brace yourselves, men! His mount's preparing to charge!"

Of one accord, every man except Antoni unsheathed his sword and raised it into the air. A few let out whoops and ran a few paces ahead, while others indulged in a little bit of fancy swordplay.

After a moment, however, one of them called out, "Hey, wait a minute, boys! We haven't had a close look at this mighty steed yet!"

Several soldiers instantly converged around the mule, and the sorry-looking beast halted. They examined it gravely, checking its teeth, running their hands down its legs.

"Just observe these rippling muscles!"

"Never knew you'd joined the cavalry, Camillus."

"When did you go and do that?"

"Well, with a sword like his, he's obviously far superior to us mere foot soldiers."

Camillus flared. "That's enough! Just leave me alone!"

"Camillus couldn't be a foot soldier anymore, boys", Ty interrupted, his voice smooth as silk. "Didn't you know that?"

Camillus shot him a look. No, not even Tiberio would be so cruel! Surely he wouldn't tell the others how crippled he really was. His anger drained and was instantly replaced with apprehension.

Ty saw his look. Oh, yes, he saw it and understood perfectly. But a smirk spread across his face, and Camillus realized that he was drunk—far too drunk—to have any idea what he was doing.

The other men were looking at Ty with mild curiosity. "Why not?" one of them finally asked.

Ty shrugged noncommittedly. "Maybe you should ask Camillus", he suggested.

Irrational panic seized him. He took a few steps back. This was no longer just a bit of drunken teasing. No, this was starting to get out of hand.

There was a silence. Everyone was watching him.

"Go ahead, Camillus", Ty urged quietly. "Show 'em your little secret."

Camillus' heart began to race. He backed away a few more paces, but the others saw his fear, and it only provoked them more. Before he knew it, three of the heftiest soldiers had grabbed him by the arms.

Violently he struggled to free himself, but couldn't. The stench of alcohol permeated the men's hot breath, and Camillus wondered how far they'd take their little game. He looked at Antoni, silently imploring him to come to his defense. But Antoni, drunk like the rest, was unmoved.

"So what's this intriguing mystery you've been hiding from us?" one of his captors asked with a malicious twinkle in his eye.

Camillus made another attempt to extricate himself from their iron hold, but in vain. The combined strength of the three of them was just too much, and he knew it.

The men glanced expectantly at Ty, who merely smiled said, "Take a look at his right leg. Just above the ankle. That is, of course, if you think you can stomach the sight of it."

The more Camillus tried to resist, the tighter the soldiers held him, their own adrenaline increasing with the struggle. Within a few seconds, they'd forced him to the ground, pinning him down. He could feel his boot being wrenched off, could feel the bandages being ripped aside. The rough treatment instantly reopened the wound, but the pain was nothing to Camillus compared with the humiliation.

A silence fell as the others stared at it, their initial curiosity changing into revulsion. Their minds raced ahead, as Ty's had a year before, to the conclusion that something so loathsome must surely be infectious.

A few backed off warily, and the three who'd been holding Camillus down suddenly released him. But as in some kind of terrible nightmare, he found he couldn't move, couldn't get up, so overwhelming was the ignominy. He could only lie there in the dirt, helpless, utterly at the mercy of his tormentors.

After what seemed an eternity, the dreadful hush was broken. It was Antoni who spoke, his voice unsteady. "You lied to me", he accused Camillus. "You told me it was nothing more than a scratch. All that time, you lied to me! We shared the same tent, ate the same food; I trusted you! And all along, you knew you were exposing me to your filthy contagion, whatever it is! What kind of a friend are you?"

No, not Antoni too! Surely Antoni wouldn't turn on him so easily! The whole world seemed against him . . . and now, his oldest friend as well! The one he'd known and trusted the longest.

Just go away, he begged silently in his heart. *Please, go away, all of you!*

As a final token of contempt, the soldier closest to him gave Camillus a swift kick in the jaw. He could taste the blood in his mouth but didn't dare move.

If nothing else, at least it broke the horrible spell. The men slowly started to disperse, jeering at him over their shoulders as they left the scene.

Ty alone remained behind, staring down at Camillus, the look on his face suddenly shameful, as if he realized, too late, the atrocity of what he'd done. He opened his mouth to say something, but Camillus turned his face away. Ty shrugged, not really caring, then departed as well, leaving Camillus finally alone.

Burning with both embarrassment and pain, he forced himself to sit up and numbly wiped the blood from his face. Then he reached for his discarded boot. He knew he should make some attempt to rebandage his leg, but as he looked at it, only hatred swelled up inside him. The ulcer itself seemed his greatest enemy; the mere sight of it mocked him, tormented him. The cause of all his life's problems.

He jerked his boot back on and stumbled to his feet. He suddenly felt that same crushing, staggering weakness that he had always experienced after some tremendous defeat in the battlefield. It was so intense it was almost physical, and instinctively Camillus reached out to the cart beside him to steady himself. He closed his eyes, waiting for the feeling to pass.

He felt a hand touch him gently on the shoulder. Someone was there beside him. He opened his eyes and saw the Father Guardian.

"Did they hurt you, my boy?" he asked.

Camillus averted his eyes, too ashamed to face him. "No", he lied. He didn't want the friar to know the truth, didn't want him to know how vulnerable he'd been against them. Pity was the one thing he couldn't endure right now.

The priest sadly shook his head. "Off to conquer the world," he said, "yet unable to defeat their own wickedness."

Camillus took a deep breath and tried to pull himself together. "They were drunk", he offered by way of excuse. "They didn't realize what they were doing."

"Indeed, a very poor justification for their cruelty."

Camillus felt drained. He could think of nothing to say.

But he didn't need to say anything. The priest could see it all in his eyes. All the hurt, the loneliness, the rejection and sadness that, try as he might, Camillus couldn't hide. It was as if the whole world had turned against this poor young man and trodden him underfoot, stripping him not only of health and fortune, but of his very dignity and self-respect.

The friar yearned to help him somehow, to give him comfort and peace. The peace the world could not know and could never give. But how? How to get through to him and offer the happiness that only the saints could possess?

"My son," he began, "listen to me. A man may live his entire life like the tide, coming and going, never constant. He's like a soldier standing in the midst of a raging battle, turning this way and that, wondering whose side he's actually fighting on." He paused, searching for the right words. "And all along, this man knows to Whom he owes allegiance, and deep in his heart wants to give it. And yet . . . yet he always holds back."

"I don't understand what you mean."

"I think you do", the priest said gently. "Our souls, Camillus, are a battlefield. And the only victor is the one who has the strength to surrender himself without reserve to his Master, our Lord Jesus Christ. Then, and then alone, will he find happiness and peace of soul. This surrender— this surrender of our hearts and wills and entire being—is a challenge worthy of the bravest soldier! It takes courage . . . the only *true* courage that our poor hearts can ever possess! Everything else is counterfeit, a mere shadow."

Courage. Camillus remembered that Curzio, too, had once spoken to him about courage. Had told him that only one kind mattered in the eyes of God. And he hadn't understood then, either.

Or perhaps all these long years he had chosen not to understand.

Was this then the same courage of which his loyal friend had spoken?

As for the Guardian, he longed to tell Camillus so much more. But alas, God alone could speak to the soul. Only God's grace could touch one's will and urge it toward Himself.

Indeed, the priest could say no more. "I shall pray for you, my son", he promised and quietly departed.

Camillus stood there alone for a long time. Finally he shook his head as if to clear his thoughts and saw that it was growing late. So much time had been wasted; he needed to return to the other monastery before nightfall. He pulled at the mule's reins.

But the animal, inevitably, refused to cooperate.

Camillus sighed, then reached to the ground for the stick still lying not far away. He hit the brute with it, but to no avail.

It was all becoming too much. Just too much in one day. Why couldn't the creature peacefully give in? Why couldn't the mule simply acknowledge who was the boss and do what it was told? It was incredible—absolutely incredible!—that after all this time the animal still didn't know what to do. Rather—Camillus amended in his mind—it knew exactly what to do, but refused to do it.

Once again, he felt his temper mounting. "Move, you stupid beast!" he ordered out loud. "You useless, hard-headed, good-for-nothing beast! Just who do you think is in charge around here, anyway?"

The mule tilted its head and looked directly into Camillus' eyes.

And in that second, it struck him like a thunderbolt out of Heaven.

Camillus was stunned. Absolutely stunned. The stick dropped from his hand, and he stood there, dazed by the force of the realization. *He, Camillus, was that mule!*

God had pulled him, encouraged him, cajoled him, even beaten him mercilessly! No, not mercilessly, he realized, but mercifully, all these years. All these long, hard, pain-filled years! And what had he himself done? He'd planted his feet more firmly on the ground each time and had obstinately refused to *budge*!

He suddenly didn't know whether to laugh or cry at the ridiculous but apt comparison.

A compelling force seemed to overtake him, and impulsively Camillus sank to his knees upon the road. With a trembling hand he reached into his pocket and pulled out the crucifix his uncle had given him so long ago. Taking it in both hands, he held it before him and stared intently at the Figure of his crucified God hanging on the Cross. Nailed there for love of him, nailed there to pay the dreadful, terrible punishment for his countless sins. And he? What had he done to cooperate with his Master? What had he ever done to return such infinite love?

A strength he'd never felt before in his life pulsed through him. He swallowed hard and tried to summon his . . . courage.

"I . . . surrender", he choked out in a dazed whisper.

His heart lifted at the words. They hadn't been so hard to say after all. In fact, they'd been the most consoling words of his entire life.

The newly found strength rose higher and higher within him, suddenly surging through his whole being with a frightful and tremendous power, unlike anything he'd ever experienced. It was engulfing him, all-encompassing, both terrifying and exhilarating at the same time. He felt as if it were consuming him, annihilating him completely!

He raised the crucifix high above his head with both hands and drew in a deep breath. Then, with all the vigor and might of a soldier charging into battle, he cried out with all his heart and will,

"I—surrender!"

He could feel the tears begin to swell in his eyes and stream down his cheeks. The overwhelming peace that flooded through him was almost unbearable! Surely it must be enough to kill him!

But it didn't. Instead, it filled him with life. And hope.

For the first time in his twenty-five long years, Camillus de Lellis suddenly knew without a doubt that he was at last a truly courageous soldier.

5. The Victory ❧

XXIX.

The Father Guardian knelt at the prie-dieu in his cell, his faced buried in his hands. He knew the knock at his door would come any minute now. He was waiting for it. *Please, O merciful Father in Heaven*, he begged silently, *let this be the right decision. Let it not be a mistake.*

At last, he heard the soft tap and looked up. His heart heavy, he rose to his feet and summoned, "Deo gratias."

At the customary words of permission, a young religious entered the cell. He knelt at the priest's feet, his brown woolen cowl still covering his head in an attitude of submission.

"Father, you wanted to see me."

"Yes, my son."

The Guardian considered for an instant whether or not he should motion for the novice to rise and be seated. No, he decided. It might be easier for the young friar to accept the crucifying will of God if he was already humbly on his knees. The Guardian drew in a breath and began.

"It has been several months now since you entered our novitiate. God's grace has wrought wonderful changes in your soul during this time. It is therefore with great sorrow that I have made this decision."

"What decision?" The bewilderment in the novice's voice wrung the Guardian's heart anew. He raised his eyes briefly to the crucifix on the wall, searching for the strength to deal this blow.

"I am afraid I cannot allow you to remain and make

your profession. The wound on your leg has worsened again; you know that yourself. It needs proper care, care that even our best infirmarians are unable to provide."

There was a silence, as the novice looked up at him. Those imploring eyes appeared suddenly so young, so alone and lost.

"I know this is not easy to accept. I have come to this decision only after seeking God's will by much prayer. You must believe me, my son. This monastery is not meant to be your field of labor."

"Then where, Father? I have nowhere else to go! I've never felt peace in any other place."

"Peace", the Guardian said gently, "is something you possess in your soul, not in your surroundings. Ask for God's light, Camillus. You know He'll help you discover what designs He has for you." He silently made the sign of the cross over his spiritual son. "Go now," he urged, "and pray. Come back to see me in a few days' time when you feel you are ready." . . .

XXX.

Camillus raised his hand to knock on the door, but held it in midair for a long, hesitating moment. Could he really go through with this? He wavered, then let his hand drop.

He couldn't bring himself to do it!

The man standing beside him gave him a stern nudge, and Camillus obediently lifted his hand again.

But he still couldn't do it!

"Go on", the other encouraged.

"I can't", Camillus said.

"Of course you can."

"It'll never work, and you know it."

"I know it won't work if you don't try."

Camillus looked at his companion dismally, but the other, realizing they were getting nowhere, elbowed Camillus aside and rapped on the door himself.

An annoyed reply came from the other side. "Enter!"

Stepping aside with an apologetic smile, the perpetrator gestured for Camillus to go in and whispered, "Good luck."

Camillus had no choice. He shot the other a last look of misery, but nonetheless opened the door and stepped, alone, into the room. He could hear the door being shut for him from the hallway outside.

To Camillus' relief, the figure seated behind the desk didn't immediately glance up. He kept working. Good. It gave Camillus time to regain his composure and gather some nerve.

He watched the man scribbling irritably on a chart spread out before him. As Camillus had dreaded, he looked busy and no doubt had little time for this interview. Camillus felt his heart sink. It wasn't going to work! The answer would be no.

After what felt an eternity, the other decided to acknowledge his presence. He still didn't look up, however. He merely snapped, "Yes? What is it?"

Camillus cleared his throat. "I . . . uh . . . I'm afraid I need your help. Again."

The man froze. Camillus knew it—his voice had been recognized. It had jarred a note somewhere in the other's memory, and no doubt a rather unpleasant one at that! Camillus watched helplessly as the man narrowed his eyes and deigned to look up.

Then he laid down his pen and slowly began to drum his fingers on the desk. *"You?"* he asked. His voice was icy cold.

Camillus attempted what he hoped was a disarming smile and shrugged his shoulders, as if his presence here was the most natural and welcome thing in the world. "Uh . . . you're the only doctor I know who can help me", he announced.

There was a frosty silence. Yes, very wintery indeed.

Camillus tried again. "Listen. I'm not the same anymore. And it's been years since—" He stopped in time. Best not to remind the doctor what had happened all those years ago!

Moretti slowly rose to his feet, eyeing Camillus warily. Admittedly, the young man did look more mature, less reckless and undisciplined.

Cautiously he asked, "Can you give me one good reason, de Lellis—even *one!*—why I should place my trust in you again?"

Camillus proffered a piece of paper. It was his only chance. "This is from the Father Guardian of the Franciscan monastery at Manfredonia", he explained.

Moretti snatched the letter but continued to keep his eyes on him for a long moment, as if Camillus might pounce. Finally, however, he lowered his gaze, unscrolled the paper, and read it in silence. Camillus held his breath.

At last the doctor raised his eyes. "I like to think of myself as a fair man, de Lellis", he said, considering. Then he waved the letter under Camillus' eyes and added, "Hmmm, yes, I daresay we'll soon see just how true *this* really is!"

* * *

Camillus reentered the corridor and closed the door gingerly behind him. He leaned against it as relief swept through him. Whew! That hadn't been easy!

From a few paces away, where he'd been discreetly waiting, the other rushed over to join him. "Well?" he asked, bristling with hope.

Camillus broke into a smile. "Hate to be the bearer of bad news, but it looks as if you'll have to bear my presence here again."

Curzio grinned back. "It'll be a penance, I can tell you that."

The ordeal over, the two old friends stood for a moment regarding each other. Curzio realized with surprise that he hardly recognized Camillus anymore. He was still the same, of course, yet somehow so very different! It was his eyes; yes, that was it. Gone was that obstinate pride, that cocky self-assuredness. Gone also were the sullen temper and restlessness that had always lurked beneath the surface, ready to flare up at the least provocation. Instead, Curzio could see a humility and self-abasement that had never been there before. He wondered what deep and painful blows it had taken over the years to make Camillus finally enter into himself and change, and the thought made him shudder.

Camillus cleared his throat self-consciously and ventured to ask, "What's the matter, Curzio? You're, uh, looking at me as if I've grown a second head or something."

Curzio hadn't realized he'd been staring. Embarrassed, he groped for words. "Of course not! It's just, well, it's just so good to see you again after all this time. That's all!"

"I feel the same."

They smiled at each other, hardly able to believe they

were truly together again, and Camillus gave Curzio a slap on the back. "Well, if I remember correctly, there's a lot of work to be done here, so let's get started."

With that, the two orderlies started to walk happily down the corridor together.

"So . . . will you tell me where you've been all these years?" Curzio asked.

Camillus hesitated. "I would," he replied, "but, in all honesty, I don't think you'd want to know."

Curzio decided not to pry. He knew that often a man had to hit rock bottom before finally being able to rise above himself.

"And you?" Camillus asked. "Have you been working here ever since I left?"

"Not quite. I went back home for a time and thought about entering a monastery, but Father Neri insisted that I'm not suited for the cloistered life. So I thought I'd better listen to him and come back here. At least until I discern what God wants from me."

"I know how you feel", Camillus sympathized. "We're both in the same situation."

They passed beneath a crucifix on the wall, and Curzio was surprised to see Camillus raise his hand in a brief salute. "Why did you do that?" he asked, bewildered.

Camillus shot him a look of mock reproach. "Curzio! Don't tell me you didn't know . . . ?" he chided. "A good soldier always salutes his Commanding Officer!"

XXXI.

It was good to sit down after a hard day's work and take the weight off his leg, Camillus decided as he pulled up a chair with the handful of other orderlies in the refectory. Things at San Giacomo never really seemed to change much. True, there were a few more dedicated workers these days, this small group of friends sitting with him at the table, but there were still so many anguished patients, alone and afraid in their death agony. So many to try and comfort, so many who ended up dying before a priest could be called.

Those old feelings had come back. The burning desire to assist them somehow through that frightful passage from this life to the one beyond. Yet how? That was the question constantly churning now in Camillus' mind. There was only so much he could do. He and Curzio, and these few others who felt the same way.

And the problem wasn't only at San Giacomo either. Indeed, by all accounts, it was reputedly one of the best hospitals in the city. What, then, of the others? And an even more haunting thought—what about the thousands of sick and poor with no one at all to care for them? Dying, alone, in some wretched hovel, or in the very streets, without so much as a roof over their heads?

Camillus' disturbing reflections were interrupted as the door flew open and Doctor Moretti strode briskly over to their table. The men glanced up; it wasn't often that the doctor sought them out here. What could be the problem?

But Moretti disregarded them all, and, as in days of old, settled his stern gaze on Camillus. "De Lellis," he snapped, "the administrators of this hospital and I have been keeping a very close eye on you lately." He tossed a sealed letter onto the table. "You needn't deceive yourself into thinking *anything* passes unnoticed!" With that, he wheeled around and departed.

Camillus felt his heart plunge. Not again! What had he done this time? He quickly reviewed the last few days. He couldn't think of any misdemeanor. His thoughts flew back over the weeks and months preceding, but again he came up blank. He was positive he'd been behaving himself.

Not that there hadn't been occasions or temptations to the contrary. Indeed, there had been all too many! He had begun to realize that conquering himself was not the work of one day, nor even a few years. No, it was a vicious battle that would doubtless rage until his dying day.

Camillus turned instinctively to Curzio. Surely he'd know if Camillus had stepped out of line! But his friend only shrugged, completely in the dark.

Camillus sighed. Oh, well, what was the use? He'd obviously spoiled his chances again. It mattered little when or how.

He pushed back his chair and stood up to leave.

"Where are you going?" Curzio asked.

Camillus shrugged. "To pack."

"What do you mean, to pack?"

"It's obvious, isn't it? I've been discarded back into the gutter, where I guess I belong." Camillus attempted a smile and assured the group of friends staring at him, "Don't look so worried. I'm used to this sort of thing."

He started to walk away, but the others protested.

"Wait a minute, Camillus!"

"Come back here."

Camillus turned around to face them.

Curzio tried again. "You haven't even read the letter yet. How can you possibly know what it says?"

"I can take an educated guess. And so can you!"

"No," Curzio said, "I can't." He picked up the letter from the table and extended it toward his downcast friend. "Don't be so hard on yourself these days, Camillus."

Camillus eyed the paper with dread but made no move to accept it.

Another orderly spoke up, kind old Bernardino Norcino. Despite the great difference in their ages, the elderly worker had become Camillus' second-closest confidant. Quietly Bernardino said, "Curzio's right. How can you expect others to give you a chance if you never give yourself one?" He shook his head and added, "In all my long years, son, I've never met a man with less self-confidence than you. You really ought to work on that."

Curzio tried to stifle a smile, but he wasn't quick enough. Camillus saw it and had to smile too despite himself. Giving in, he returned to the table and took the letter from his friend.

The others moved in closer and watched as he unfolded it and read the contents in silence.

He blinked, uncomprehending, then narrowed his eyes in concentration. Was he reading this correctly? Suddenly he felt the need to sit down again, and dropped into the chair, his eyes traveling to the top of the script and starting all over again.

"Well?" one of the orderlies finally urged. "Tell us! What does it say?"

As if in a daze, Camillus began to read the letter out loud. "Dear Doctor Moretti, we are pleased to inform you that your request has been approved to have Signor de Lellis . . ." he paused and glanced up, incredulous, at his small group of friends, "appointed General Superintendent of San Giacomo Hospital."

XXXII.

The instant Curzio opened the door he could see his timing was bad. Camillus was sitting at the desk, staring at the jumbled mess of paperwork spread out before him with a confused frown. He didn't seem to notice his friend's entrance.

Curzio cleared his throat and softly scolded, "What are you doing back in here? Doctor Moretti told me he gave you strict orders to stay in bed and not to move."

Camillus looked up absently. "Oh. I thought I'd better get up again. Too much work to do."

Approaching the desk, Curzio studied him closely. "What's wrong? Are you getting sick, or what?"

Camillus made no reply. He obviously wasn't listening.

Curzio took the paper out of his hand and repeated the question. "Are you sick?"

"No, I'm not sick."

"Is your leg bothering you again?"

"No. Not that either."

Curzio could tell he was slightly embarrassed. "Then why did Doctor Moretti send you to bed?" he persisted.

Camillus snatched the paper back and replied, "It's nothing. I just managed to pull a few stomach muscles somehow. Don't worry about it."

"You pulled a few stomach muscles?" Curzio raised a quizzical eyebrow. "How did you—"

But Camillus interrupted him. "Have a look at these accounts here, Curzio. It's taken me weeks to realize what exactly was happening here. Some thieving scoundrel has been pilfering from this hospital, left, right, and center, under my very nose!"

Curzio sat down on the edge of the desk and studied the pages Camillus was holding. "That's an awfully high price for an order of thirty-two bags of flour", he commented grimly.

"It certainly is! But that's not even half the problem!" Frustrated, Camillus let the papers drop. "The bill *says* it's thirty-two bags every time, but do you know what they've really been delivering?" Without waiting for an answer, he continued, "Twenty-two bags! I did a surprise inspection down in the storeroom this morning just as the dealer was leaving. He seemed to have, uh, accidentally misplaced ten entire bags. And I finally got those two chicken-livered orderlies downstairs to admit he's been misplacing them for months!"

"Neither of them had bothered to report it to you?"

"Of course not! They've been pocketing their filthy portion of the profit."

Curzio let out a low whistle. "No doubt the hospital's down two orderlies?"

"But that's not all!" Camillus went on, warming up. "When I insisted on opening one of the bags, what do you think I found? —the high-grade flour we've been paying for . . . or the low-quality muck I canceled months ago?"

Curzio shook his head. "I don't envy your position. Sounds as though there's a fair amount of corruption in this hospital."

"You're right about that. I'll never be able to straighten it all out if I live to be a hundred." But it only took a moment before Camillus' anger drained, and he bowed his head into his hands on the desk. "But do you know what I did about it, Curzio?" he asked, suddenly starting to burn with shame.

"Uh-oh. I'm not sure that I want to hear."

"You guessed. I did it again. I lost my temper! I *really* lost it!" He looked back up, and Curzio could see he was truly contrite. "I opened the door and personally threw every single bag of flour out into the street."

Curzio stared at him, stunned. "You threw twenty-two two-hundred-pound sacks of flour out the door?"

"Well . . . yes", Camillus admitted sheepishly. "But that was only after I . . . oh, never mind." He stared at his desk top with despair.

"After you *what*?" Curzio demanded incredulously.

"After I . . ." Camillus grimaced at the memory and continued miserably, "threw the dealer out first. I suspect I might've truly hurt the man . . . knocked out a few teeth, or, um, broken his nose, or maybe—" He looked up with sudden amazement. "What are you laughing at?"

To his dismay, Curzio was starting to shake with barely controlled laughter.

"Stop it, will you? It's not funny!"

"You're right," Curzio managed to choke out. "It's not! It's hilarious!"

Camillus could only watch him helplessly. After a few moments, however, the laughter proved contagious, and Camillus joined in as well, although less wholeheartedly and with more than a little pain.

Finally Curzio got a grip on himself and took a deep breath. "Don't worry about it, Camillus", he assured his friend gently. "I'm sure God has already forgiven you. Where would the merit be if we didn't have to keep on fighting?"

"I know", Camillus admitted with a heavy heart. "I was so upset about it afterward that Doctor Moretti gave me a choice. Either a triple dose of one of his revolting tranquilizing potions, or a stern talking-to by Father Neri. Naturally I opted for the latter."

"And he told you the same thing?"

"More or less." Camillus shook his head regretfully and changed the subject. "So, why did you come in here, anyhow?"

"I just had a little favor to ask you. But never mind. I can see you're far too busy."

He stood up and headed toward the door, but Camillus ordered, "Come back here! I'm not *that* busy!"

"Oh, really?" Curzio indicated the disorganized clutter all over the desk with amusement. "You call this not busy?"

Camillus looked down at the untidy stacks in front of him and frowned. Then, with one motion of his arm, swept the entire mess off the desk top. Curzio watched in horror as the pages fluttered through the air and scattered to the floor.

"There", Camillus said with a satisfied grin. "Not busy at all, see? What's this favor you're after?"

Curzio closed his eyes and groaned. "I can see this hospital's in one very sorry state with you sitting behind the main desk."

"You're absolutely right", Camillus agreed. He tossed his friend an ingratiating smile and suggested, "Maybe they should have made me a doctor instead and been done with it. What do you think?"

Curzio laughed. "That's not such a bad idea. At least you treat the patients with more mercy than you do the poor contents of your desk. Or innocent sacks of flour, for that matter!"

"What's this favor?" Camillus persisted.

Curzio's expression sobered. "It's about a patient who was admitted a little while ago. I thought you might be able to help him." He hesitated. "The man's a soldier. He's in a bad way. Doubtful he'll even make it through the night. Lost a couple limbs. I have no idea how his friends even got him this far. . . . The journey should've killed him. Bernardino and I have been trying all evening to console the poor fellow somehow, but he simply refuses to talk to either of us. So I just thought, if anyone could get through to him, it would be you."

"Has a priest been called?"

"Yes, he received Extreme Unction practically the minute they brought him through the door."

"I don't know if I can do any better than you, but I'll try my best." Camillus abruptly rose to his feet. But the sudden action caused him to double over with pain. Aghast, Curzio realized that Doctor Moretti hadn't ordered him to bed for nothing. He reached out and quickly grabbed his friend before he collapsed. Then he carefully eased him back into the chair and waited helplessly for the agony to pass.

"Which . . . ward . . . is he in?" Camillus managed to get out.

"Forget it! The only place you're going is back to your bed, where you belong!"

Camillus stubbornly pulled himself up again, although with considerably more care and less speed this time. "Which ward, Curzio?"

"I said forget it! You're seriously injured! Why didn't you tell me?"

"I did tell you."

He said it with such genuine innocence that Curzio

found it impossible to be upset with him. He shook his head and explained patiently, "There's a considerable difference between simply pulling a few stomach muscles and rupturing half the inside—"

"I don't know the difference."

Curzio changed his mind. Just as well they hadn't made him a doctor after all.

"Tell me where he is."

No answer.

"You might as well tell me. Because if you don't, I'll just have to search the whole hospital, won't I?"

No point in even trying to argue; Curzio knew he was defeated already. "Ward eleven", he gave in miserably. "But Camillus, please! You're really hurt. Doctor Moretti will have my head for this."

"No, he won't", Camillus promised. "If he does, I'll fire him."

Curzio couldn't resist a laugh. "Small consolation," he returned, "but thanks anyhow." Then, shaking his head, he asked, "What did I ever do to deserve such a rogue of a friend as you?"

"I don't know, Curzio, but it must've been pretty wicked. And I thought *my* past was bad! Now, are you going to help me to get there, or do I have to go alone?"

* * *

The dim light of early dawn had barely started to brighten the room when Curzio made his way back through the rows of beds. Even from a distance one glance sufficed to tell him that the soldier had been dead for several hours already. But Camillus was still sitting on the edge of the bed, his expression dazed and stricken. He didn't even look up at Curzio's approach.

"You've been here all night, haven't you?" Curzio reproached softly.

Camillus didn't move for such a long time that Curzio wondered if he'd even heard the question. Finally, however, he raised his eyes, slightly disoriented. "I . . . guess I have", he admitted numbly. He shook his head as if to clear his thoughts.

Worried, Curzio sat down next to him. "You're really upset about this, aren't you? I had no idea it was going to affect you so much. I'm sorry. It's all my fault."

"Nothing's your fault. I'm fine, honestly."

But Curzio didn't think he looked fine.

"It just brought back a lot of memories, that's all. How could I have forgotten so easily? There are so many of them like this, Curzio. You have no idea. Hundreds of them, just left out there on the battlefields to die. Alone. With not even a friend to be there with them." It took an effort for him to go on. "Simply all alone! Surrounded by nothing but bloody corpses, heaped around them, at times even on top of them, and so afraid to die." Camillus couldn't continue. He tore his gaze away from the dead soldier's face and bowed his head into his hands.

Curzio sat there helplessly, longing to say something, but not knowing what.

"I want to go back out there and help them," Camillus said at last, "but I don't know how. The only ones who mean anything at the moment of death are priests."

"Did you at least get him to talk to you?"

"It took a while, but yes."

"Did you ask him his name?"

"Why would I ask him that?"

Curzio looked down at the dead man on the bed with

sorrow. "Never mind. I don't always remember to ask them either", he consoled gently. "But somehow it just makes it sadder when there isn't even a name to pray for."

Camillus raised his head and looked at him, uncomprehendingly, for a long moment. Finally he seemed to realize what Curzio meant. "You misunderstood me", he said. "I didn't have to ask the man his name. I already knew it."

"You mean he was a friend of yours?"

"Not exactly. But maybe he is now." Camillus looked up. "His name was Dario", he said. "Dario Tellini."

XXXIII.

From his shady spot under the tree, Father Philip Neri could see the approaching figure along the lakeshore and carefully closed the pages of his breviary in expectation.

"Ah, Camillus," he said with a welcoming smile, "I see Doctor Moretti has finally unchained you from your bed and let you loose."

Camillus groaned. "After weeks of confinement."

"Well, my boy, I certainly hope you've learned your lesson."

"Yes, Father. Believe me, I won't be losing my temper again in a great hurry!"

"Come, sit", the priest urged, patting the grass next to him.

Obeying the command, Camillus added, "But it gave me a lot of time to do some serious thinking, lying in bed all those weeks." Then, changing the subject, he gestured toward the fishing tackle on the ground under the tree. "Any luck?"

"Luck!" Father Neri repeated, feigning offense. "You

need more than luck on this lake, my boy! Such timing; such delicacy of touch! In fact, quite an array of skills . . ." He paused, winked at Camillus, and admitted candidly, "Absolutely none of which I possess!"

They both laughed, but then the priest's expression sobered. "Now, no one would come all the way out here just to listen to the mindless prattling of an old cleric, so there has to be another reason. Of what serious things have you been thinking, Camillus?"

Camillus hesitated, unsure how to broach the subject. After a moment he began, "In your opinion, Father, is there a place in the Church for a group of men . . . uh, possibly religious . . . who could devote themselves to the care of the sick and dying? I mean, not for wages, but for God. Solely for the love of God."

"In my opinion? A place, yes, indeed. And more than just a place—a definite need!"

"Exactly! That's what I was thinking!" Camillus burst out with sudden confidence and enthusiasm. Then, in an excited rush of words, he blurted out his idea. "See, I've been thinking lately that if I . . . or, rather, not me, because I wouldn't have any idea what I was doing! But if you were to help, then perhaps a group, or a congregation, or . . . or something! . . . could be formed to fill that need! And it could do so much good because so many people die all alone and have no one to assist them and—"

"Wait! Slow down!"

Sheepishly Camillus closed his mouth and noticed with dismay that Father Neri's eyes were twinkling with amusement. The good priest drew in a breath and began logically, "That's all very commendable, Camillus, but first we must pray, to know if it is indeed the will of God. An undertaking of this nature will require a little more than five minutes' preparation, you know."

"But . . . but you started the Congregation of the Oratory," Camillus reminded him with genuine confusion, "and it's flourishing."

"No, Camillus," Father Neri corrected gently, "I didn't start the Oratory. God did. And He makes it flourish! He simply uses whatever useless tools are to be found lying around His workshop." He shook his head and chuckled reminiscently. "Oh, dear me, the young Father Neri, of himself, could no more have founded a religious order than the old Father Neri could supply the markets of Rome with fresh fish."

Camillus had to laugh. His spirits rose a bit again as the saintly Father continued in earnest:

"This proposition may very well be in Heaven's designs. Yet I think it best if it were to be guided by . . . a priestly hand."

He looked straight into the other's eyes and added, challengingly, "*Camillus?*"

Instantly Camillus' face fell, and he lowered his eyes. He shook his head in refusal. It wasn't as if the thought had never before entered his mind. To the contrary, he'd pondered it many a time in the last few months. But invariably he'd come to the same conclusion.

"With *my* past, Father? You've got to be joking", he said at last.

But Father Neri was undaunted. He only shrugged and countered cheerfully, "Saint Augustine became a bishop!"

"Yes, but Saint Augustine had at least paid attention to his studies."

To his surprise, the old priest's voice suddenly took on

an authoritative edge, and he commanded sternly, "Very well then, Camillus. You must make the time to go back to school yourself, and *pay attention!*"

XXXIV.

Curzio wondered if he'd ever get used to seeing the black cassock. He always felt as if he had to look twice to convince himself that it truly was his old friend wearing it.

This time, however, a second glance wasn't really out of order. The priest descending the church steps could have been any of dozens in this area of Rome. But fortunately Curzio could recognize not only Father de Lellis' size, but also his gait, even from this distance. It had become obvious over the last few years that the mysterious wound on his leg simply would never heal.

"Father, wait!" Curzio called out, quickening his step.

Camillus turned around and waited patiently for him to catch up. Then, raising an amused eyebrow, he asked, "Coming from the docks again, Curzio?" He shook his head reprovingly and teased, "Really, you must choose your companions with more discretion."

Curzio made a face at him. "My companions, thank you, happen to be entirely above reproach. I doubt a poverty-stricken old gentleman and his blind granddaughter are going to be a source of corruption. But, by all means, I'll introduce them to you, if you insist on monitoring the influential characters in my life so closely." He paused, then added seriously, "As a matter of fact, Father, I'd really like to introduce them to you. If you have time, that is."

Camillus feigned a menacing look. "Do so, or else."

"All right, but not just now. There's another thing I want to talk to you about first."

"Fire away."

"You've been keeping secrets from me, haven't you?" Curzio accused as the two started to walk toward the hospital.

"No, I haven't", Camillus replied. "You know I wouldn't do that. I just wasn't quite ready to tell you yet, that's all."

"Well, news spreads quickly at San Giacomo, and I've already heard. At least, I think I have. But I still want to hear it from you. So, go on. I'm listening."

Camillus grinned. "Do you remember that problem we once had? Well, actually still have."

"Of course I remember."

"And you told me to find a solution for it?"

"Well, have you?"

"I'm not sure. I hope so. But first, Curzio, let me tell you a little story that my father used to tell me. I've never told it to anyone before, because I never knew what it meant. He never knew either." Camillus paused and seemed to be thinking back to distant memories. At length he began, "My mother was a very pious lady. At least all the villagers thought so. When I was about to be born, she had a very hard time, until, by some inspiration, she asked my father to carry her out to their stable. He did, and apparently I was born straight afterward. But then, Curzio, she had this vision. And she had it over and over again until the day she died."

"A vision?" Curzio was listening with awe. "What kind of vision?" he asked.

"She used to see me leading an army—a huge army—of black-robed soldiers with red crosses on their hearts."

Camillus grinned. "Of course, my father and I liked to flatter ourselves that I was destined to become a great military general someday. But, well, I admit our hopes were shattered when I kept getting kicked out of every army I joined. So Mother's dream obviously meant something else."

"What about her?" Curzio asked. "What did she think it meant?"

Camillus had to laugh. "To be honest, I was such an unruly child that the vision terrified her. She was sure it foretold something terrible!"

Curzio smiled. "I can understand that. What do you think it means now?"

Camillus hesitated. "Well . . . I hope I'm right. I've decided, if it's God's will, that is, to try to—"

But Curzio was too excited. He had to have the satisfaction of finishing the sentence himself. "To start a religious order to nurse the sick and especially the dying! Am I right?" Without waiting for an answer, he stopped walking and raised his hand in a sharp military salute. "Because if I am, then I'm your first recruit!"

Camillus was caught off guard. He knew it should have been the other way around. How mysterious were God's ways! He, too, stopped walking, and a smile spread across his face. Nonetheless, he tried hard to make his voice sound authoritative. "Curzio, three things", he said. "First, *this*—", he reached out and lowered his friend's saluting hand, "is not for me, *ever*! Second, if an order is founded, it will only be because God wills it. I have as much chance of starting something like that as I do of, well, catching fish."

At Curzio's quizzical smile, however, he dismissively explained, "Never mind. Just a figure of speech."

"And the third thing?" Curzio ventured.

"The third thing. Guess what I'm going to call it!" Camillus smiled triumphantly and answered his own question. "The Servants! The Servants of the Sick!" He looked hard at his friend, and, for the first time in all these years, Curzio could see the old fire start to blaze in Camillus' eyes as he added, with almost frightening determination, "And do you know what's more, Curzio? One of these days, I'm going back into those battlefields again! Not to shed blood this time, but to bring the Saving Blood to those who so desperately need it!"

Somehow Curzio felt sure that Camillus had never said anything with such heartfelt conviction in all his life.

"Well, I can promise you right now, you won't be going there alone," he returned, with equally blazing eyes, "because this time, Camillus, I'm going with you!"

Camillus tossed him the first cocky smile he'd seen in years and asked, "How did I know you were about to say that?"

Then he threw a comradely arm around his loyal friend's shoulders, and Camillus de Lellis and Curzio Lodi, the first two Servants of the Sick, went on their way together.

Afterword

In his lifetime, Father Camillus de Lellis established fifteen religious houses and eight hospitals throughout Italy and other parts of Europe. His "vast army of black-robed soldiers" consisted of more than three hundred spiritual sons (Curzio Lodi being the first, and old Bernardino Norcino the second), who, in addition to the usual vows of poverty, chastity, and obedience, bound themselves to a fourth: to seek out and nurse the sick, even the victims of the plague. As a result, many of them died in their heroic work of mercy.

The followers of Camillus were the first ever to wear the famous Red Cross on their clothing, and, under the protection of such a badge, they ventured into the very battlefields to assist the wounded and the dying.

Camillus de Lellis passed to his heavenly reward in 1614, after attaining great sanctity and working many miracles. His body remained incorrupt in Rome for eighty years, until the flooding of the Tiber River caused its decomposition.

In 1746, Pope Benedict XIV raised the penitent ex-soldier to the honor of the altar, declaring him a "saint of the Holy Roman Catholic Church" and establishing his universal feast on July 18.

He was later declared patron of the sick, of hospitals, and of nurses.

Of Brother Curzio Lodi it has been said that he nursed the sick with such charity and untiring devotion that angels were seen administering to them at his side. He became so gravely ill himself that he was forced by holy obedience to leave the order and return home. After a convalescence of two years, however, he was finally well enough to rejoin Camillus, and he remained a faithful Servant of the Sick until his death in 1602.

Author's Note

This story was originally written as a screenplay for a movie. Although never produced, the script formed the framework upon which this book, first published in 2001 by Lepanto Press, was written. The text has been slightly revised for this new edition.

For those readers who find themselves curious about how much of the story is true: I assure them that the events and all the major characters in this book are firmly based on fact. The only notable exception is Doctor Moretti, whose character serves to personify the entire medical staff at San Giacomo Hospital. Likewise, Dario Tellini has a fictitious name and a fictitious death, although there was indeed a soldier with whom Camillus fought a duel.

As to whether the future saint was still hospitalized in Rome during the Battle of Lepanto, and whether he at one time hired himself out to the Turks, historians disagree. I have chosen, in both cases, to adhere to what the majority of biographers seem to believe. If I have erred in either of these regards, I ask the reader's indulgence, as I hope to have that of Saint Camillus himself as he looks down from above.

At any rate, as all historical novels are an intricate blend of fact and fiction—and this one is no exception—my intention was not to write a scholarly biography; rather, I simply wished to tell the inspiring story of one of my close friends in Heaven.

If this short novel makes Saint Camillus some new friends as well, then I shall consider my efforts amply rewarded.